Praise for TiGeorges' Chicken

"It feels good in here. It tastes good in here. And congratulations on your dream coming true in Echo Park." —Huell Howser, *Visiting with Huell Howser*

"All hail the king." —Jack Boulware, *American Way*

"A wonderful restaurant." —Evan Kleiman, *Good Food*

"There are people in this world so passionate and with such a positive, infectious attitude that it carries over into everything they do. TiGeorges, the owner and operator of TiGeorges' Chicken in Los Angeles is one of those men." —Noah Galuten, *Chowhound*

"The Haïtian-style conch, lambi, at TiGeorges' Chicken near downtown may be just the thing." —Jonathan Gold, *LA Weekly*

"A place of roast chicken, fricasseed goat, vanilla-spiked limeade, and coffee roasted with sugar until it smokes." —Charles Perry, *Los Angeles Times*

"The inimitable TiGeorges Laguerre is Haïti's unofficial ambassador to LA, moving fluidly from table to table, painting his native country as an enchant̶e̶d̶ ̶i̶s̶l̶a̶n̶d̶ certainly tastes that way at his re̶s̶ —*Los Angeles Mag*

D1466827

"The coolest little spot...home to wood-burning rotisserie chicken." —*LA Weekly*: Best of LA 2004

"Real good Haïtian food." —*Carib Press*

"Haïtians, and lovers of Haïtian food in California, wake up! It's time to get your Haïtian chicken at TiGeorges' Chicken restaurant." —*Haïti Observateur*

"A little piece of Haïti, in Los Angeles...Above all, the sweet plantains." —*La Opinion*

"Succulent chicken...Nifty little establishment." —*Gayot*

"Finger-lickin' chicken, bold flavors, and fresh ingredients." —*LA Press*

"TiGeorges' Chicken takes Haïtian barbecue seriously... spinning Georges' succulent chicken to juicy perfection." —*The Guide*

"Attractions include the restaurant's jovial proprietor and a soundtrack of irresistible Haïtian music." —*Los Angeles Times Magazine*

"Georges is Haïti's happiest, giving us a glow we usually blame on too much sun." —*Blackbook*

"TiGeorges' effervescent, eponymous downtown LA dining joint is one of the best places to come for fine Caribbean dining in California."

—*Los Angeles Daily News*

"The result is, as the French would say, *formidable*."

—*New Times LA*

"Smother TiGeorges' rotisserie chicken with the special Haïtian garlicky vinegar sauce and you'll be happy. The conch sauté are especially tender and you might want to order an extra sweet potato pudding, because if you're not alone, your friends will eat it." —*Metromix*

Los Angeles Downtown News: Best of Downtown 2007

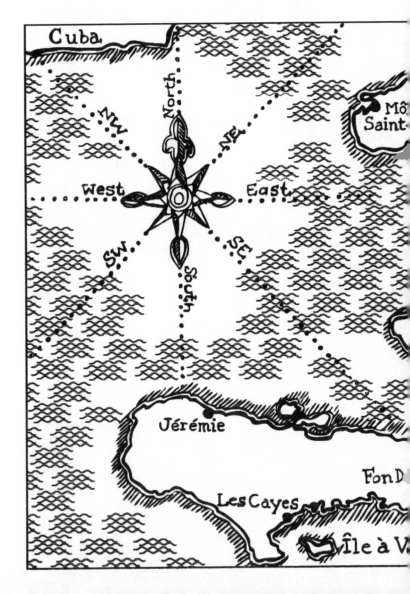

AN ISLAND

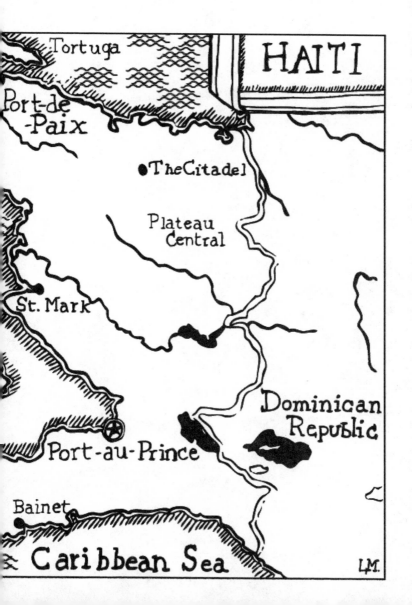

Tortuga

HAITI

Port-de
-Paix

●The Citadel

Plateau
Central

St. Mark

Dominican
Republic

Port-au-Prince

Bainet

Caribbean Sea

LM.

A Genuine Rare Bird Book

TiGeorges Laguerre

NO MAN IS AN ISLAND

with Jeremy Rosenberg

A Memoir of Family and Haïtian Cuisine

This is a Genuine Vireo Book

A Vireo Book | Rare Bird Books
453 South Spring Street, Suite 302
Los Angeles, CA 90013
rarebirdbooks.com

Set in Minion
Printed in the United States

10 9 8 7 6 5 4 3 2 1

Publisher's Cataloging-in-Publication data

Laguerre, TiGeorges.
No man is an island : a memoir of family and Haitian cuisine / by
TiGeorges Laguerre; as told to Jeremy Rosenberg.
pages cm
ISBN 9781942600251

1. Laguerre, TiGeorges. 2. Haitian-Americans—Biography. 3.
Immigrants—Biography. 4. Haiti—Social life and customs. 5.
Cooking, Haitian. I. Rosenburg, Jeremy. II. Title.

E184.H27 .L34 2015
972.94/06092—dc23

To my friends growing up:

Alix-Raymond, Georges E. Laguerre, Reginald Pierre, Georges Pierre, Lys Joseph, Remy Joseph, Seraphin Élibert, Leaman-bien-Aimé, Ronald Boulos, Carle Bouzi, Vladimi François, Marc-Albin Laguerre, Sothenes P. Philippe, Heinz Valcourt, Marc Antoine Fenélon, André Louis, and Walner Thervil

CONTENTS

FOREWORD

By Charles Perry

I N THIS VIVID, CONVERSATIONAL autobiography, Georges Laguerre wants to show Americans another side to Haïtian culture beside the clichés of poverty and voodoo. His Haïti is a place where people run businesses and picnic at the beach, and country boys get dissed at big-city high schools.

He tells the story of a remarkable family, governed by an amazingly determined grandmother who ordered them all to move to Brooklyn and make their future in the United States—though none of them spoke a word of English at the time. (The grandmother herself, who stayed in Haïti, did know two English words: "fresh fish.") It was a rocky transition, but the children all became successes. Georges himself has landed on his feet several times in his life, saved by his hustle and enthusiasm.

Naturally, it's also a story of food—Haïtian food, which he forcefully argues is not just "West Indian food." (In fact, there's no such thing; every Caribbean island has its own culinary dialect.) Each chapter revolves around a kind of food, and he gives away a lot of the secrets of his restaurant, TiGeorges' Chicken.

And when he tells you how to cook a goat, he starts with how to butcher it. So this is a practical book, not just a good read!

—Charles Perry, Los Angeles

INTRODUCTION

By Jimmy Jean-Louis

ERE IN CALIFORNIA, THE Haïtian community is very small. I've lived in the state for about ten years, and it's with great thanks to TiGeorges that I've been able to maintain a connection with my homeland, my country, and my roots.

I do this through the food TiGeorges Laguerre serves, and most of all, I do this through his wonderful spirit.

When TiGeorges' Chicken opened, it became *the* place where Haïtians would go and meet, have some *real* Haïtian food, speak the language, and feel like we are back at home. All that taking place in a little pocket of Glendale Boulevard near downtown.

What else can I say about TiGeorges? He's so full of energy! I think the business is *him*. The business is who he is. He brings a passion to his customers, to every recipe, and to everything he does. The way he carries himself—as a proud Haïtian man—is something I can relate to.

I'm an actor. In my business, being black and being Haïtian on top of that is not easy. In TiGeorges' business, it's the same way. I know how hard he's working, I know how hard he's fighting. He's fighting all kinds of people and all kinds of notions. He's fighting spirits and powers just to be able to make a culinary and cultural statement.

And TiGeorges Laguerre is succeeding! The man deserves all the acknowledgments and raves he receives. As a Haïtian, I'll always be there, proud to support and push him. I'll always encourage the other brothers and sisters from Haïti to do the same. And not just Haïtians—everybody! Because this man is just exceptional at what he does.

—Jimmy Jean-Louis, Los Angeles

PREFACE

MY NAME IS JEAN-MARIE Monfort Hébert Georges Fils Laguerre.

You think my restaurant meals are a mouthful, try saying that long name.

I mean it. Try saying it right now, whether you're reading this on the bus, on the subway, at home in bed, or on the sofa, or if you're out here in Southern California, say it as you're sitting on a beach, waiting for the sun to set, your mouth watering thinking of the Haïtian meal I'm going to prepare for you tonight.

So do me this one favor: say it with me, not for my ego's sake, but to get to know me better—to really truly understand that in the Americas, they don't give names like this anymore: Jean-Marie Monfort Hébert Georges Fils Laguerre.

I received such a long moniker because I died at birth. Truly. The priest administered last rites. Then an injection brought me back, with the only side effect a youthful limp. In the meanwhile, the doctor, the nurse, my mother, my father, and in retrospect what seems like every other resident of Port-de-Paix, Haïti, was adding their own memorial contribution to the baptismal certification that our city's hospital was preparing for me.

And the funny thing is, with all those names, I'm best known by something else entirely. People call me TiGeorges. That's pronounced "Tee Georges." It means "son of Georges"—as in, my father's name was Georges. And by the way, Georges is pronounced "George," as in President George Washington.

I set out to prepare this book as a counterbalance to all the horror stories about Haïti that people outside the country have heard. Yes, Haïti has been for some time a troubled land. But if you're looking to read about political upheaval and plague and pestilence and, worst of all, some weird voodoo zombie nonsense, let me tell you: this ain't the book for you! I want to introduce people here in print to the same glories of Haïti that I recount with each restaurant serving. The beauty of the country. The pace of life. The kindness, generosity, and civility of most all of Haïti's people. The human connectedness still so prevalent there. The sea. The spirituality. The potential.

As you read the pages and chapters ahead, you'll learn much more about my family—for instance, that I was one of ten brothers and sisters. You'll learn more about my journey, which began in Haïti's Northwest, pressed on to Brooklyn, and continued across the continent to Los Angeles, California, where I've resided for more than thirty-three years. What else do you need to know up-front? I have two great sons, Benjamin, born in 1990, and Michael, born in 1993. I was married for thirteen years. I speak four languages. I've been an entrepreneur and small business man—but alas, not a filmmaker—ever since I graduated from college. And since 2001, I've had the pleasure of being the proprietor of a restaurant that's about way more than just food. Cultural connector, melting pot, history and geography lesson, quadrilingual hub, TiGeorges' Chicken is way more than the sum of the items listed on a menu. Read on, and I hope you'll see what I mean.

Okay, please excuse me now. You hear that popping and sizzling, grease dripping off rotisserie chicken? You smell that avocado wood smoking, indoor cooking that recollects the best of outdoor barbequing? You see those customers arriving, some speaking Kreyol, some English, some Spanish, some French, everyone excited to eat? Let me tell you: I've got to get back to my kitchen! Come join me here in Echo Park.

Enjoy the book.

A NOTE ABOUT THE EARTHQUAKE

ON JANUARY 12, 2010, a horrifying, devastating earthquake leveled much of Haïti—and in particular, the capital, Port-Au-Prince. Haïti is home to some eleven million people. By some estimates, more than three hundred thousand people perished due to the quake. That's nearly three percent of the country's total population. Unbelievable. Unimaginable. Please forgive this macabre comparison, but to put that figure into perspective, God forbid, if three percent of the people in the United States died, that would mean about six million people! Imagine how many of those people you would be acquainted with. Think, too, about all the people who you'd know who'd just lost their homes and their jobs. After the quake, in Haïti, at least one and a half million people—that's about fourteen percent of the population—were at least temporarily displaced.

The rest of this book is not about the earthquake. The world knows enough about the problems of Haïti, and not enough about the joys of the people, the place, and the culture. This rest of this book is also not about the electrical fire that hit the exterior signage on my restaurant and caused my business to be closed for so very long. This was a tough blow for many reasons, including that the restaurant is one of the few West Coast gathering places for Haïtians and friends of the Haïtian people.

After the fire, when the restaurant was closed for repair, I put up these words on my old-fashioned, analog marquee: "Reopening soon!"

On a much greater scale, and over a much longer timeframe, the same will happen in Haïti. Haïti, in its post-earthquake years into decades, will reopen for business, man! Haïtians, the Haïtian diaspora, and the people of the world will—for whatever their personal and business reasons—work together to make this country a place for everyone to be proud of. That's not naiveté—that's coming from someone who has made a lifetime out of knowing, seeing, working, and— whenever I can, same as so many of you—helping.

On a deeply personal level, I'd also like to thank everyone in Los Angeles, and people elsewhere far beyond, who took such a positive interest in helping the people of Haïti during the days and weeks and months after the earthquake. From the hundreds of people who packed our post-earthquake fundraiser, to people contributing to the new nonprofit we've started, to the outpouring of well-wishing, supplies, and financial relief, I'd like to just take this moment to say thank you.

And to all my friends, family, and countrymen and -women back in Haïti—hang in there. Five years later, the going is still slow and sometimes it is easy to submit to the significant frustrations and obstacles of the moment. Especially when that moment seems to last a lifetime. But we must stay focused. And we must not abandon hope and hard work. Haïti will rebuild bigger, stronger, and far better.

ENTREÉS

THE ISLAND COMBO

A Haïtian experience—one quarter or one half chicken, rice with beans, salad, *plátanos fritos*, *pikliz*, and *acra*.

Garlicky, citrusy, wood-burned rotisserie chicken.

That's what I aimed for. And it wasn't easy.

It took me four years to build TiGeorges' Chicken. Before I had the restaurant, I built a barbeque grill in my backyard. I set it up by myself, learning as I went. I had to build a spot where I could dispose of the ashes. I also had natural gas burners where I could barbeque and cook some other things simultaneously. And I built a sink.

I practiced and prepared on my own. Then it was time for a more public taste test. I cooked two chickens. I invited my very good buddy—an Italian guy called Attilio—my neighbors, and some other people to let them know what I was going to serve at my restaurant. Well, let me tell you: to my surprise, the food was good!

Well, I shouldn't say to my surprise because hey, I damn well knew how to cook. But I didn't expect quite the great taste, the great flavor that came through.

That was 1997, when I didn't yet have the money to build a restaurant. I was a year removed from an unhappy marriage. Whatever I wanted, that's not what she wanted. I've always been a businessman because I grew up in the business world. My dad had his own business, my mom had her own business—later in life, she was also a nurse. My grandfather was a mayor. My grandmother, again, a businesswoman. She was very strong, and basically was the one who educated all of us. We were ten brothers and sisters.

My grandmother loved me so much when I was young, in part because I was a sick kid. She always wanted to protect me. She always made sure all us kids ate well. And she was blunt, too. I was probably eight years old when she said, "Come over here, son, I want you to know something: your wife will be the first one to fuck you."

Oh! At the age of eight to have your grandmother telling you things like that!

"You know, your wife is going to give you dirty words," my grandmother said. "Your wife will do mean things to you. Your wife one day will not cook for you. And I'm going to make sure that you know how to cook, how to press, how to wash, how to do all of life's basic things."

So, great! I loved the idea. I remember my grandmother going to our city's open-air market. She would grab me by the hand and I would go with her, and she would buy me a small cooking pot like you would buy for a little girl. And hey, I didn't mind that. I was with my grandmother. I loved her and she always showed me love. It was beautiful. Ours was such a powerful relationship.

Other boys were playing with guns and arrows. I would be sitting next to my grandmother, cooking a smaller version of the day's dinner. She would kill the animals out in the back, especially goats. One time she said, "We're going to change our routine." She had killed another goat—no, what's the name of that animal again? Lamb? Well, in French we say *moutoun*. So she killed that particular animal. Oh man! You know moutoun is not really in the culture of Haïti. I mean, even today I know of very few people there who consume lamb. But my grandmother killed one, and then she fixed it. And guess what? None of us would eat it. "Oh, okay, you guys don't like it." That was all she said.

Life was forever interesting with my grandmother. I remember my brother Harry, he loved to go fishing. We lived two blocks from the beach. And my grandmother always said, "Young boys do not stay in bed after 6:00 a.m." So we all had to get up early. Regardless if it was raining, hailing, you name it—well, in Haïti there is no hail, okay?

But we had cold—oh yes, Haïti does get cold. If you do go to the capital, Port-au-Prince—my dad used to take me there and it would be cold. And that's a big difference. I mean being in Haïti, especially in Port-de-Paix where we lived, the temperature would be one hundred degrees and then your dad takes you to an environment where it could be thirty degrees. *Whoa, whoa!* Let me tell you: that is the part of Haïti where they cultivate apples and all the other fruits that require two temperatures, hot during the day and cold at night. Like grapes, for instance. Once upon a time, someone told me that Haïti has the capacity to make wine like Bordeaux, France. One day, I'll have enough money to be independent, to have the freedom to move about and to produce wine in Haïti.

For now, though, making wine is a much more difficult proposition, requiring more money, more equipment, more focused time than are available to me. I did try growing limes. In 1997, I went to the Dominican Republic. I was crossing the border and I saw big trucks full of lemons and limes going to Haïti. Haïtians consume these foods, but Haïti doesn't cultivate them in sufficient amounts. I thought, *This is truly a shame. We have the same capacity the Dominicans have. Why is Haïti not able to do this?* So I set out to do something about this. When I returned to Los Angeles, I called growers up in central California to see if I could buy any seeds to bring to Haïti to cultivate.

One grower said, "Of course! Look at this, it costs only five dollars." I thought, "Wow, this is really cheap. I'm ready to go." The lady selling the seeds said, "Well, you're going to have to wait for the right time." And she had to explain to me how farmers should wait for the appropriate temperature. They should wait for the crop to fall off the tree. And then wait to process the seed. "It's a long process," she said. "You have got to wait." I waited like almost three or four months. And then at long last, she said, "Yes, Georges, I got the new seeds."

So I planned and then I planted. I went to Haïti and put the seeds in little pods, and I called everybody in the neighborhood where I grew up. Hey, many of them were my cousins! I wanted to show them, "Listen, this is serious, together we're going to make a change, together we're going to make an impact." Then I returned to Los Angeles and waited a year. I went back to Haïti and saw that basically, yeah, there are some lime trees there. But it was not yet a big business. And even my own cousins were unwilling to put in the hard work required to take on this kind of enterprise. This, sadly, is an all-too-typical attitude among educated Haïtians. I'm not giving up, though. To do this right, I will need a lot of money. I will have to buy or lease more land. So like the vineyard, this is another project I'm putting back on hold. Don't think I won't get it done! I think in the long term, and I persevere.

Don't believe me? Then you've never been to TiGeorges' Chicken. So let's talk now about poultry and preparation. How do we do it at TiGeorges? The short version: We use a custom spit. We cook right here inside the restaurant. We use a special kind of felled, savory wood. You'll read much more soon about all that. When we put the chickens on the rotisserie, we slow-cook 'em. We keep the smoke to a gentle waft, we don't burn the skin, we hit that perfect copper color, smooth texture, and succulent flavor. We're talking about an hour and a half on that spit before we can even think about finishing my chicken.

When I first started out, when I'd just opened the restaurant, there was a guy passing by every day on his motorcycle. After he became a regular customer, he told me that he'd been desperately trying to figure out where this incredible aroma was coming from. Here in Echo Park on Glendale Boulevard where my restaurant is located, people are usually driving their cars in high gear, going fast, never having the time to look around. But guess what? After a while, the smell of my cooking brought that man on the bike to my front door. And since then, I've had him as a customer. And let me tell you: he's not alone!

Ahh, the smell! Cooking is not just about putting the chicken on the grill. No. First, we marinate the chicken with the spices that Haïtians use, mainly chives or green onion. And garlic—we are great believers in garlic. We are great believers in thyme. We also use tomato paste. But since I do a rotisserie chicken, there's no use for tomato paste. In my case, I replace the tomato paste with paprika. Paprika gives us that color I'm looking for. We also add a dash of wine, so its sugar content enhances the meal's signature texture.

When I was a kid back in Haïti, my family was fortunate enough to afford maids. Louisine was my favorite. Her name, for the non-French-speaking readers, is pronounced "Louis-een." Truly she was a master. I picked up so many culinary techniques from her. She would, for example, never burn or overcook her meats. She would boil them, then put that meat over a grill fire, then pour on the gravy, and then put the meat back in the oven to re-juice the gravy. Because gravy is not soup. So often, people come to my restaurant and they expect the gravy to be watery, or the gravy to contain flour. No. In Haïti, we do not put flour in our gravy! We reapply the same juice that's come from within the meat. That's the reason for the quality of gravy that I deliver every day. It's a very basic Haïtian staple.

I don't know how much any of you know about making candy. Anyone who knows about making candy knows that you've got to know when to stop. Well, the same process goes for gravy. You've got to wait until the sauce starts bubbling. It's going to be bubbling as if it's frying—but it is not frying. That is the key, that's when you know the gravy is ready. Otherwise, if it's watery, if it's making large bubbles, then you're not going to have a great gravy yet and you need to continue reducing. Trust me, you go the Haïtian route, you're going to end up with quality gravy.

You want to know another technique of mine? One that I've received a good amount of attention for? Well, let me tell you: TiGeorges' Chicken cooks with avocado wood.

Avocado wood comes in layers, just like an onion. When the fire starts, it starts with big flames, but soon the fire is going to reduce to a lower temperature. In order to bring that fire back, you've got to constantly keep your eyes on the logs, and you've got to constantly poke them. If you don't poke that avocado wood, then it's not going to give you the flame you need. It depends on how well-dried the wood is. If you use wet wood, then of course you're gonna end up with a lot of smoke and a lot less heat. Every day, I fill my restaurant's pit three-quarters of the way full with wood. Then I light the fire and wait forty minutes. Then it's time to place the chicken on the rotisserie.

Now, this all took trial and error to perfect. Remember, this rotisserie grill was my design. Sure, I tested the prototype that I built in my backyard. But the one that I have in my restaurant is an entirely different beast, a far more advanced machine because we're cooking indoors not out. I'll confess: I was never one hundred percent certain I could pull off this technique of recreating inside a storefront space that magic formula from outdoors—that magic that ran, as you'll read, from Haïti through Texas and on through to Glendale Boulevard. But it happened! The taste exceeded even my goals for flavor and style. And when it came to code, the city officials were satisfied too. My rotisserie, my oven vent, my kitchen, my entire restaurant, was approved by the Los Angeles Health Department. This was January 23, 2002. It was really truly a dream come true.

☼ ☼ ☼

To THIS DAY, MORE than a decade later, there's no one else in town that does what we do. Usually restaurants that spit-cook chicken do it so the rotisserie is enclosed; it's separated from the dining area or stuck behind some glass case. But at TiGeorges', the rotisserie is right in the heart of the dining area. On many occasions, people arrive curious to see if indeed I'm really using wood to cook the chicken. I show these people around with pleasure, showing them my tricks, my private techniques, like how I keep the fire going by setting up a fan on the bottom part of the barbeque.

People ask me all the time, "Is this rotisserie chicken setup reminiscent of life back in Haïti?" Yes and no, I tell them.

Yes, in that back in Haïti we used to dig a hole, a barbeque pit—you know, like the Hawaiians. In the mountains, especially, we'd do this. And it's also a

Haïtian thing in the sense that we're forever grilling in Haïti, especially good meat. We either fry meat or we put it on a grill. We'll dry the meat and then we'll barbeque.

But what I do at TiGeorges' Chicken is basically convert that tradition and, like I said, bring the outdoor indoor. That's what makes the difference in my style of restaurant. What you're seeing here is also Haïtian, of course, because I'm a Haïtian! But if you go to Haïti, you're not going to come across people cooking in this fashion. Because everyone in Haïti—even if they reside in a fancy hundred-thousand-dollar house—cooks outdoors.

Early on, I was worried that all of this might turn out to be a huge mistake. Business was not always great. There was a Thai restaurant across the street. Let me tell you: people would line up for their cuisine. And here I am, a nice smoking barbeque grill, offering hearty portions, a good price, and a charismatic cultural experience, and shit, nobody is coming. I'd focus on winning over one person at a time—like that guy on the motorcycle. Or like this other man, a shorter, older Spanish speaker who grew up in the neighborhood. He wanted to come in. He didn't want to come in. Maybe he should come in. He had mixed feelings about my restaurant from the get-go.

I thought, *I really need this man as a customer.* Well, guess what? That same thought reached his mind, and finally he walked into the place. He pointed at the spit and said, "I want this chicken." And I said, "No, the chicken is not ready." He said, "It looks good, I'll take it. Give me that chicken." I wanted so badly to please him, so I pulled off a chicken, split it in half and gave it to him, and he departed. About half an hour later, the guy came back. I had a couple of other people in the restaurant. Man, this was one of the most embarrassing moments of my life. This guy—this symbol of neighborhood acceptance—loudly announced to the room, "Excuse me, could you tell the man back there that the chicken he just gave me is a raw chicken! I want my money back. The chicken is not even cooked!"

Whoa, man, in front of my few customers! Let me tell you: I felt so bad. I said to him—and really, to myself—"You want to know something? I will never ever again serve the chicken directly from the grill. Everything now is going to be done the Haïtian way."

So since that episode, a TiGeorges' chicken, once it's finished cooking on the grill, it enters into the oven along with the same juices it was marinated in, and with some olive oil added—I truly love olive oil. The end result? No more half-cooked debacles, and instead, a really truly hybrid Haïtian and American sensation.

LAMBI

PEOPLE COME TO MY restaurant and want to talk about *tonton macoute*, voodoo or *vouduon*, Papa Doc and Baby Doc Duvalier, things of that nature. Those are the only things that people claim to know about Haïti. To which I say, "Well, wait a minute!"

Haïti was the first country that was able to fight the French. The first black republic! Haïti set an example! What I have witnessed is that very few people—even people who have received PhDs—know any of these stories.

So my job here in the restaurant is to open people's eyes, to feed them information. To let them know that of course Haïti is part of the continent of North America, and that in 1492 Christopher Columbus disembarked in Haïti. Very few people know that. In the States, it's often said that Christopher Columbus disembarked somewhere in the Caribbean. But for some reason, people never mention that it was Haïti. But it was. When you go to school in Haïti, this is among the very first things you learn.

Here, they teach about Columbus and the "West Indies." *No no no no no.* That's the reason why my menu and my sign outside both read, "Haïtian cuisine"—I truly want to separate myself. Because when you say West Indies, you're generalizing, you're talking about Jamaica, Puerto Rico, Cuba, the Dominican Republic. No. I don't want to be generalized. Haïti played a very important role in the making of the modern world.

So for people who say, "Haïti is in the Caribbean or is part of the West Indies," I say, "No!" Well, okay, Haïti is in the Caribbean, but Haïti has something very different to say than the rest of those islands. Like I said, one of those differences is that Haïti fought the French. And not only that, but Haïti has been occupied by the Spaniards *and* by the French. Basically, we have so much more history than those other islands. Haïti is the only country in the Americas that has its own language, which is Kreyol.

People will say to me: "Do you speak patois?" I find that offensive. Because it is not a patois for the Haïtians. It is a language. This is how I communicate. Everybody in the country speaks it. There is grammar. There are books—just like French, English, or any other language. As a matter of fact, Kreyol is such an interesting language that it not only it has its own grammatical code, but a lot of body movement as well. When you watch a Haïtian talking, you will see a lot of body movement and hand gestures. To the uninitiated, this can be intimidating. No. This is how we are, how we express ourselves. It is nothing to fear. In Haïti, you'll find groups of us gathered at a corner, and usually we will be talking about stories from other lands. What's been taking place in Europe, in Africa, in America. This is what we Haïtians normally do when we gather together.

Another thing we do when we gather is, of course, eat great food. Let's move back to that topic.

Now, there is something that we consume in Haïti that we call *lambi*. A lot of people, reading that French word, think that it's lamb, as in a parent of a goat, a cousin of a goat.

It is not goat. It is not red meat. No. Lambi is conch. It comes from the ocean. It is a cousin of abalone. Oyster. Clam. New Zealand mussels. That's what it is—a very tough meat. And for almost everyone who comes to my restaurant, I have to explain that. I don't have any problem with that! I love explaining things to people. Because my style of cuisine is still new to most Los Angelenos. We have to explain in detail exactly what's in our meals, and what customs and traditions are related to each food.

For instance, we Haïtians consider lambi to be an aphrodisiac. I was a little bit reluctant about including that bit of information on the menu, but my older sister Marie said to me, "Hey, Georges, it is a reality. This is something that exists in the Haïtian culture. And if you fail to put it in there, you are cheating yourself."

Me, I tend to impress girlfriends with my cooking. I make such great meals that on many occasions I've had girlfriends who want to come for a repeat. "Hey, Georges," they say, "When will you cook me again that best dish you fixed?" As a matter of fact, I remember I was dating this girl and I fixed some New Zealand mussel. Let me tell you: she said, "Georges, you definitely turned me on."

Even my dad, he kept a jar of marinated lambi beside his bed. As a kid, though, I didn't yet know why.

☼ ☼ ☼

AT THE RESTAURANT, I'LL tell customers about all this and they'll say, "Georges, is that true? How could you certify a thing like that?" I'll say, "Listen, since my childhood, this is what I've seen and been told." And look, there's a belief here in America that eating oysters will enhance your sexual appetite. Oysters and lambi— they are cousins. Kissing cousins? Perhaps more.

Lambi. Let me tell you: in Haïti, picnics usually take place by the beach. You've got the ocean breeze so temperatures are a lot cooler seaside than inland. So say you're on a romantic picnic and since you happen to be in the neighborhood where lambi can be harvested, well, do you get my drift? Take advantage of the moment because lambi cannot be harvested everywhere. There are few countries in the world that can harvest lambi. Haïti is one of them.

In Haïti, there are several ways we fix lambi. We barbeque it. Then again, we can do it as a fricassee. We roast it. We mix it with rum—preferably rum that is made out of sugar cane. However you gonna do it, you'll need heat. On the beach, people usually set cooking fires with found wood. Remember, when people on boats or elsewhere dispose of trash out at sea, it washes up on Haïti's shores. When you go to the beach in Haïti, you'll find plenty of lumber.

My restaurant is located near the man-made Echo Park Lake, and not the Pacific Ocean. TiGeorges' Chicken isn't Haïti, and we cook our lambi very differently. Lambi is tough, it's not a tender meat. You have to tenderize it. You have to mince it, make it into very small pieces. Then boil it. Normally this takes about three hours. In my restaurant, once it's been boiled I then prepare individual or table-sized portions. But this is not the norm in Haïtian culture. There, we'd prepare a larger batch, put it out, and serve it to all comers for the entire day, or until the plate is empty. But since we're in America, I don't prepare lambi in a single whole batch. We have refrigeration, we have freezers. We have patience. And when we dine out, we like to have menu options, not just one available item. So when you walk into my restaurant and order lambi, you will have to wait, yes, but you will not have to wait too long.

Now, how do I prepare the lambi? I sauté garlic. Add oregano. Then parsley, lime juice, and black pepper. A little bit of paprika and habanero chili. Then olive oil—you'll read over and over again that I'm a great believer in the flavor and the health benefits of olive oil. By the way, I know some people enjoy raw garlic, but not me. Roasting really brings out garlic's flavor. Okay, so mix all of the above together. Then roast some onion, or shallot for those who prefer. Then bell peppers. When these have been roasted, that's when you'll put in the lambi. It will have the juice and everything needed already in there. Add a little bit of salt—not too much salt; remember, this food came from the ocean so it naturally has some salt. Now do the oregano again and a little bit more lime juice. Sauté everything together and let it reduce. If it's too watery, you're not going to accomplish anything. You don't want to make soup. My style of cuisine, I'll say it again, is not soupy. Reduce the juice!

My restaurant's walls have photos, prints, and maps showing Haïti. So much of what I can share even today about the nation's geography comes from what I learned at home, as a kid. My dad made sure that my brothers and sisters and I could draw on a piece of paper the boundaries, the shape of Haïti, with our eyes closed.

Like I mentioned, I'm from Port-de-Paix, which is in Haïti's Northwest. The island of Tortuga is right across from where I grew up, but believe it or not, I've never been there. My uncle Abner swam that channel between Port-de-Paix and Tortuga. Let me tell you: we talking about swimmers in my hometown? I couldn't swim, and I can recall very few good swimmers. But my uncle Abner was one of them. There's another guy by the name of Jean-eli Teifor. He married my cousin Elsie, and he's an artist, one of the top Haïtian artists. He was a guy who really could swim that channel. I remember seeing him in the morning and he would say, "Well guys, you can walk to the beach and I will meet you on the other side." By the time we would get to the beach, he'd be there. I'd estimate his was about a two-mile swim.

My father was born in a place called Bainet, down in southwest Haïti, to the bottom left of our wall map. My dad always wanted my siblings and me to go meet his family. I was probably twelve or thirteen years old when my dad put me and my brothers Michael and Taylor on the bus to go meet my uncle Tijuana. We'd spend summers with him and my cousins. That was great fun, to get to be with them and hang out together.

I'm looking now on the map at Port-au-Prince. That's the capital of Haïti, and where most of my aunts live. Like Aunt Emmeline, and my cousins Norma and Grim. Most of my father's side, they live in either Bainet or Port-au-Prince.

Where else should I mention? How about Plateau Central, an elevated area in the middle of the country?

There's a lot of water there and, subsequently, rice cultivation. Let me tell you: Haïti definitely produces a great quality of rice. My mother operated a general store—and bakery—and she used to travel to Plateau Central to purchase the rice she'd then sell.

Let's see, where else? How about in the north, where the Citadel is the eighth wonder of the world? You go to Haïti, it's important you visit the Citadel because that's where a lot of the battles took place that made Haïti the first black independent nation. I took a photograph near there of a beautiful woman selling mangoes at a roadside open-air market. More about that later.

How about we mention one of the nicer destinations in Haïti? It's called St. Mark. It has white sandy beaches that were never too crowded. When we'd travel to Port-au-Prince, we'd ride along the coast and encounter this spot. It's wonderful, with cliffs as well as that white sand. Another place people like is called Jérémie, which is farther south, and is known for its French colonial architecture and its collection of poets and other freethinkers. Then there's Gelé, farther south. The Haïtian global diaspora gathers here annually for festivals that last a week or two. If it's mid-August and you are looking for a Haïtian expatriate you haven't seen in decades, visiting Gelé is your best chance to encounter them. Either that or Facebook.

I should also mention Île à Vache. Many Americans who visit Haïti, for some reason, love that location. It's an island, about three miles off Les Cayes, surrounded by the Caribbean Sea, and it's a very attractive place with a nice beach. And the soil—it's a very reddish looking soil, like you were in Arizona or Kenya. Very appealing. Very interesting. And then there's this other interesting place called Fon Des Blanc. The name means "the skin," "the white skin." This is where many Europeans used to live. Most of the Haïtians who reside there are very light-complexioned people. They are almost about the color of the soil, because of the mixture of the red, the white, and the black. And then of course you will see people with green eyes and black hair. Haïti is truly a mixed society! You'll find Palestinians, you'll find Spaniards, you'll find Americans, you'll find French, you'll find Canadians. We're all mixed.

Finally, I want to mention Môle Saint-Nicolas, which faces Cuba. I don't know if it was in my imagination, but as a kid, I always believed that I was able to see the smoke rising from the factories producing sugar in Havana. Maybe that's just my mind being mischievous. But certainly, there is a raft of connections between Haïti and Cuba. For starters, I truly believe that many of the blacks who live in Cuba are Haïtian descendants. More personally, my cousins and uncles on my mother's side used to work in Cuba. They'd take the boat from Port-de-Paix. They used to work in the morning and would return to Haïti in the afternoon or, more likely, at the end of the week.

Music is another tie Haïti has with Cuba. At my restaurant, every Saturday the band Los Puros plays live. Los Puros, they play classic Cuban songs, Cuban songs I remember listening to on the radio. Growing up in Haïti, especially if you're in the Northwest part like I was, you'd receive all these great Cuban radio stations. Let me tell you: I feel so good around these guys, the Los Puros guys, because they feed me. It's like they come to work so happy, just like me. It's almost like magic. And customers who come to watch, they'll refuse to leave. And if I'm not here to hit the conga or say some stupidity on the microphone, or maybe even sing, then the regulars will ask for me. Yes, really truly, I do get up and sing, and people say I'm good at it. People say, "Hey, you look good doing this." Well, the songs that the band plays are old songs, forty- or fifty-year-old songs. Songs I used to hear as a kid. After all this time, you know all the lyrics, you know all the movements. So in the eyes of some people who hear me, they'll think I'm a musician. But if you bring me newer music, something fresh that I don't know, the truth is, I won't do it so well.

Another Cuba-Haïti connection was the lotto. In Haïti, lotto was a big thing. We had something called *bolet*, known also as fifty-fifteen-ten. As in: fifty *gourdes*—which was ten or so US dollars—would be the first prize. Fifteen gourdes, second prize. Ten, third. The winning numbers we took straight from the Cuban lotto. It happened every day, usually twice a day. Some people get lucky, most people don't. Just like any lottery. People would listen to the radio for the Cuban songs, and then for the Cuban lotto numbers. I remember kids, those that couldn't speak Spanish fluently, they would think that the radio announcer said number "sixty-five" versus "seventy-five." *Se-sen-ta y cinco* as opposed to *se-ten-ta y cinco*. This caused some problems. I would hear guys say, "*No no no no no!* That's the number they said!" Yeah, right. There were probably people who lost an arm or a leg because they didn't understand the language.

This was not a government-run lottery. Anybody in Haïti could do it. I could go tomorrow and establish myself as a *bolletier*, a ticket seller. And some people made themselves a small fortune. Even as kids, everybody played. There were no age restrictions. It's not like here where you've got to be twenty-one years old. I would go put a gourde on the stuff—which was a dime, or no, it was twenty cents. I never won. But if I had, I'd have ended up with fifty gourdes. That would be ten dollars. Back then that was a lot of money.

CABRIT

LET ME MAKE YOU a list of the top ten foods of Haïti.

The list consists of *legume*.

Of acra.

Of rice and beans.

Of something called *djon-djon*, which is mushroom.

Salted fish.

Corn meal with red beans.

Oh, and something called *bouillon*. Bouillon is a soup. This is something that is very popular, something that goes hand in hand with *fritay*—pronounced "free-tie"— which are basically fritters that people cook on sidewalks and sell on streets, usually at night. Yes, fritay, and yes, bouillon, which is usually made out of goat meat.

In the town where I grew up, there was this lady by the name of Ismelia. She was really truly an expert at cooking goat meat. Any manner you like to enjoy your goat meat, Ismelia was the lady that you wanted to know. Not only was her food going to be good, her food was going to be healthy, and her food was going to be clean.

Another item on our top ten list is lambi.

And, of course, *griot*. I'm sure if I didn't at least mention griot—which is pork—some Haïtians out there would be very unhappy with me. You go to any restaurant in Miami, New York, even in Haïti, griot is big, definitely. They may not have chicken, and they definitely won't have rotisserie chicken, but for sure, griot will make the menu.

I think this list has gone past ten foods, but we'll have to continue! We're yet to reach *cabrit*—goat. Ask me about the best meal I ever ate back home, and let me tell you: it was goat.

There's a fashion in which we consume goat in Haïti. When we kill the goat, we make a stew with the feet, the head, the intestines, the liver, all of that. In mainstream America, this is not considered appealing. But in Haïti, when you can find someone who can prepare goat stew, definitely, this is gourmet for Haïtians. *Gourmet*.

I remember one Christmas, just before I came to America. Our neighborhood friends and us would chip in, whoever had money, and we would buy goods for a party. One of the guys, by the name of Briant Louis, his mom prepared the meal. That was definitely the best goat meal I've ever had. It had to be 1968, because in 1969 I left my hometown and went to Port-au-Prince to study, before I came to America.

Why was that one goat so tasty? In part because it's always exciting to eat at a party. And in this case, to eat thanks to a friend whose family seldom cooked for the rest of us, so we didn't have any expectation of such high quality! Briant Louis's mother really truly came through—her dish had such flavor and such tender meat.

Usually in Haïti, you buy live. You take the goat home and do the butchering, sometimes the day of the meal and other times the day before. That's what Brian Louis's mother did. Then she prepared goat stew. Goat stew. I mean, it's spicy, it requires a certain sensibility. It is not made for everyone. Goat carries a very unruly smell. But Haïtians, we kill that smell—you've got to wash that goat with a lot of hot water, with a lot of lime, and you've got to let that meat sit and marinate in the lime. I'm almost certain the acid in the lime kills some of the smell and some of the bacteria and makes goat a healthier, tastier food.

Incorporating brains and feet and the like, you'd think that'd make the stew tough. But no—not after we tenderize. This is something that we start doing very early. If the goat happens to be killed in the morning, then that stew wouldn't be ready until four or five in the afternoon. It's a long process to clean and cook goat. Back in the sixties, everything was done outdoors. It would be fire, peat fire. Now today, okay, some people have begun to use indoor cooking, but then outdoors was the lifestyle.

So with the goat, you begin preparations by washing, just like I explained on the Huell Howser show. What? Some of you don't know Mr. Howser? Then you really truly don't live in Los Angeles. I'll tell you more later about his wonderful public television program and all that it did to help my restaurant.

Anyway, there are, let's see, one, two, three different ways that I prepare goat. We'll focus here on roasted goat. You'll need a big pot. Goat's a very hard meat, it's not tender. Some people add tenderizer, but I don't use chemicals in my food, so I'll tenderize naturally. Put the meat in the pot, add water, and let it boil until the water reduces. When the water finishes, then you're going to have fat starting to drip, just like on the rotisserie spit. The whole idea of roasting the goat is to remove the fat. Not only that, but remember, the fat itself is going to cook the meat. It'll look like the meat is burning because the bottom part of it is going to stick to the pan. That's because we put bell pepper and a whole bunch of spices down there—let's say, onion, chive, garlic, habanero chili, and parsley.

Once the sticking starts, then pour in a little more water. Any time you pour water, you'll need to stir. Then cover the pot and continue frying, but don't let it burn again. You gotta keep your eyes open, pay constant attention, okay? Then add a little bit more water, pouring it on the outskirts. Don't pour to the center, because that's where most of the meat has been glued and stuck on the pot. The water has two functions: it steams, allowing the meat to disconnect from the pot, and it provides more color.

Haïtian food is very colorful. If I'm invited to a house in Haïti, and the meat is not well-cooked or it doesn't have any color, or it is *white white white* meat, or it doesn't have any tomato paste, or isn't basted with something that gives it color, well, I'm going to question it. I'm going to say, "You didn't really work with that meat." The whole idea of giving meat color is to certify that it has been thoroughly cooked, and that you have really truly worked with it to make it good and really give it taste. So go stir that goat for half an hour to forty-five minutes. The time varies depending on the intensity of the fire. If you're using a household burner, plan for extra time. If it's a commercial burner, though, beware. Commercial burners deliver more intensity, more heat. Anyway, you'll go through that process about five or six times. At some point, you're going to see the meat changing color. And hey, remember, as you water and steam and stir—you don't want the lid always off and the flavor all escaping. But then again, you do want to let your neighbors smell the good food that you are cooking! Let them say, "*Oooh.* My neighbor is cooking something good. *Hmm,* maybe I should kind of stage myself, or go pay my neighbor a visit to see if I may be offered a plate of food?"

If you're not going to serve the goat right away, put it in a cooler. Goat contains a lot of fat, which you'll see immediately at the top of the pot. You can use a spoon to remove ninety percent or so of that fat. *If* you are going to serve ASAP, then add olive oil to replace that removed fat. Add some more onions or shallots, too. And, oh yeah, one last thing to consider. Goat, it's not prime rib. Goat, it's not filet mignon. Goat, it's not T-bone steak. Goat has a lot of bones. I know a lot of people will go to the supermarket and say, "I want the leg or the shoulder—all meat, no bones in there." You know something? It's not going to have the flavor, the taste that you want. Because the flavor also comes in the bones, okay? You're going to want to put your finger in there when you're eating, okay? You need to go in there and dig, really fish for the meat. And you gotta have time to enjoy, to savor, the good goat. Don't be intimidated! Go to the supermarket and ask the butcher to give you meat with bones! I know here in the society that we live in, if it has bones in it, it's not the greatest. No. *Au contraire.* Remember, we are doing something cultural.

Now there are other ways of making goat. We can dry and fry. Or we can mince. If we're drying, that'll take a day or two, depending on the weather. If it's the rainy season in Haïti, we're not going to have much sun. Once the goat dries, we'll fry it, making fritay. In Haïti, we all do it. We eat supper at home and then we go out later and buy food cooked by other people, and sold by vendors on the sidewalks. Even a millionaire, if he doesn't go out at night himself, he'll send the maid out to bring him some fritay.

When we're serving fried goat, we consume it along with fried plantains. We cook by double frying. We fry the plantain first. Then we dice it—don't make too thick of a dice. Then we refry. Once the food floats in your pan—in my case, I used a deep fryer—then you know it's almost cooked. Let the food float for an extra minute or two to make sure the inside is properly done. Then set the stuff to the side for a minute or two and then crush it flat. Then dip it into salted water and dump it there again in that frying pan. Then, enjoy the meal.

☼ ☼ ☼

By the way, goats are tremendous animals. Anyone with a backyard that needs to be mowed? Bring a goat and I guarantee you that fellow will tear your yard apart. In Haïti we always have to curb our goats, because if a goat gets in your backyard, trust me, the goat will eat any plant, you name it—expensive flowers, anything. They are very good for that. I even wonder if domesticating so many goats in Haïti has contributed to our loss of trees?

I mentioned earlier how rank a goat smells. Well, to be fair, people aren't always so much better. In Haïti, we believe that the body chemistry of the chef has a great impact on the taste of the food. I know it sounds controversial, but this is our belief. This is the reason why some people in Haïti cannot cook: because their bodies emit a noxious odor. If you emit an odor that is not appealing to other people, then I guarantee you, in the Haïtian cuisine, your cooking, the taste, the quality, will never be what you're hoping for. You're laughing at this? This is not a joke. Let me tell you: as a kid, we had a maid who suffered from this unfortunate problem. I think it's unfair to mention her name because she was very nice to me. She was fair, she protected me, but yet, she was someone who could never cook, could never deliver the quality that Louisine used to deliver. For that simple, very factor: this lady mingled her odor into the food. When you'd pass her by, you'd have the sense she hadn't showered. The same held true for her food—even the rice somehow seemed unwashed. I know I'm disclosing something that most Haïtians will not discuss publicly, but it is truly in fact something that exists in Haïtian cuisine.

We are all born with certain talents. I don't think malodor is something that can be one-hundred-percent corrected. I'm sure with modern technology you can go and have operations and have certain things removed from your body. But I'm talking about my past experiences in Haïti, when I was growing up, about how we looked at people who were involved with cuisine in the kitchen. Well, remember, in Haïti, let's say, our minds were closed. Closed in the sense that we were never really truly totally curious about delving into certain areas. But here in America, because this is a modern world, people will question everything. But when I was growing up, the idea of openly questioning other people about their body chemistry? Didn't happen.

I know this lady who used to sell fritay. I mentioned her name, Ismelia. She carried a nice aroma and so too did her cuisine. Ismelia had a competitor—or a potential competitor. This lady, her food was never good, she had such problems selling. Why? You guessed it—body chemistry. We taste food as much with our nostrils as we do our tongues. By the way, my cousin Norma, she would watch how this other lady couldn't sell any food and at the last minute, like at ten or eleven at night, Norma would go out and buy the biggest, best fish she could still find. She'd fry it up and go challenge that one lady's sales spot. And Norma would really clean up. She never dared cut into Ismelia's business, though. Just one fish, fry, and sell.

Here's another example. TiGeorges' has photos and prints and maps on the walls, like I've said, plus some newspaper clippings of articles written about the restaurant. One of the prints really illustrates the sixties Haïtian lifestyle. I'd love back then to ride on buses just like the one depicted here. I'd take a transport just like this when I'd go from the province to the capital.

Now, my uncle on my father's side was named TiJean. He was a great driver. I remember him driving those big trucks! I'd say to myself, *How could someone*

possibly drive a vehicle of that size on a road that narrow?
TiJean was expert, he was well known for hauling cargo.
All the top businessmen of Haïti relied upon him to
deliver goods. Like cacao, for instance, or any other
product cultivated in the south and then delivered to
the capital and then sent overseas.

In the illustration on the wall, in the lower right
corner, there's this cart with a sign that reads, "Fresco."
A *fresco* is basically a snow cone—grated ice blended
with flavored syrups. Oh, there'd be so many honeybees
flying around that syrup, and the fresco man never
really chased them away. He must have been quite
used to those bees. Also in the illustration, a little
kid is dancing. Now this truly brings back memories.
Childhood. Summertime in Haïti. Heat. Humidity. Let
me tell you: some days, I'd hang around and consume
five or even six fresco*s*.

Also in the illustration is a young man playing a kind
of drum we call *tambour*—it's like a conga. The guy is
dressed in blue jeans and a hat and a red scarf, typical for
how a peasant would dress during carnival season. This
scene here was playing out in an environment where
the local culture had been preserved, not corrupted by
other cultures, which is taking place in Haïti today. You
will find the European culture is becoming very strong,
the American culture, Andean culture—basically,
influences from around the world. But this picture
really describes what Haïti was once like and, to some
extent, still is like.

The main object in the picture isn't the drum player or the snow cone man. It's the wild, cobbled-together-looking bus. Vehicles like these would transport a mix of passengers and cargo. See how everything is made with wood? This isn't the New York subway, there isn't metal and hard plastic straphangers. These vehicles were modified by hammers and nails and maybe every now and then, okay, a welding torch. You ever read that book or seen the film *The Grapes of Wrath*? Well, these buses in Haïti, we call them *tap-taps*, but in this country during the Great Depression, you'd have called them jalopies.

How these buses were able to climb mountains, I'll never know. Overloaded with goods and people, every side and rear view obscured, and the Haïtian roadways sometimes mottled or muddied or just plain disintegrated. There was one notorious driver named Lil' Rousseau. He used to work an eight-or-so-kilometer route from Port-de-Paix to a place called Shansolme. He worked for this older guy by the name of Pére Levier. Lil' Rousseau was a very aggressive driver. The guy would probably have two or three accidents per year. On occasion the trucks would flip over, and, thank God, people would never really truly get badly hurt. And then guess what? The guy, Pére Levier, would continue giving the truck back to Rousseau to drive.

On Rousseau's vehicle, and in the print we've been discussing, you see passengers jammed inside the bus, and you also see everyone who prefers to ride up on top, where the cargo is. This was the best way to travel, because you could see the surroundings. Also, let's face it, with at least some breeze up there, you wouldn't have that foul smell that surely would come from at least one of the passengers down below. I mean, what did we know then in Haïti about deodorant? I'm not trying to insult my people but it is a true fact. For me, deodorant was something that I only become accustomed with here in America. I had a valet parking job in New York City. The gig was to move cars from the Sheraton Hotel at Fifty-Seventh Street and park them at Fifty-Fifth Street and Eighth Avenue. I was a young guy, it was okay for me to run four or five blocks to get a car. After a while, though, running, if you didn't wear deodorant—well, one day, the owner of the parking lot, he said, "Georges, you know something? Tomorrow if you're coming back, you're going to have to find a way to wear deodorant."

Alright, I'm switching topics now. I want to speak more here about Louisine, who was our incredible maid and a true mentor. She is incredible. Let me tell you: when Louisine fixed something to eat, it was superb on all levels. She was a great culinary teacher, as well. We'd be trying to prepare something and she'd come by, have a taste, and say, "Oh, okay!" It would mean a lot to get an approval from her. But then again, when she was on occasion mad, she would report my siblings and me to our mother: "They were doing this," she'd say. "They were not doing that." And Louisine had so much power, so much influence, regarding all of my brothers' and sisters' education. Where my mother would not tell me no about something, Louisine would. She had the courage, the discipline, and, somehow, the household authority. For example, my friends would come to hang out, and Louisine would shoo them away. "Hey, you're not supposed to be here. Don't you have a house? Why don't you go home?" She would not allow my friends at dinnertime. Of course, there's poverty. Most of our friends did not have what we had, and often, yes, they would come hang out because they wanted to enjoy the meal that my family would enjoy. But Louisine would not tolerate that. She would say, "*No no no no*, this dinner is prepared for the family and I'm going to ask you to leave." Most of my friends didn't like her. She was a very tough lady. She's still alive, very old.

Ahh, Louisine. The family would always finish eating the meals she'd prepare. But another way I learned my cooking skills would come later at night, when my brothers and sisters and I would want a snack. If we didn't go out for fritay, then we'd fix something ourselves. We'd wait for my parents and my grandmother to go to sleep. And then we'd start cooking. This would be at like 9:00 p.m., which in Haïti felt late. That was because you didn't always have electricity—probably the grid was shut off by 8:00 p.m. to conserve. Back then, it was like, no electricity? No problem, let's go for a walk under the moon. Let's go to a party on the beach. Or let's just go to sleep. Me, I'd light a candle at home and start cooking. My siblings and I would fix rice with you name it. Rice with red beans. Rice with herring. Rice with *bacalao*.

We'd cook, we'd eat, and guess what? We wouldn't wash the pot that night. So who is going to encounter that pot first thing the next morning? Louisine. She would say, "Oh, you guys cooked last night." And then we'd have to be especially nice to her in order to keep her from telling our parents. You always had to be on Louisine's good side.

She was very good to us, she cared about our health. Once, my brother Michael was very sick. My mother was always busy. Although she trained as a nurse and later, in Brooklyn, worked the graveyard shift at Florence Nightingale Health Center, in Haïti mom operated a general store and a bakery. When any of us didn't feel well, Louisine would notice first. And if my mother wasn't in a position to take us the hospital, then Louisine would do it. I remember one day when Louisine said to my mom, "Ma'am, Michael is not feeling well. I think you should call the doctor." And because of our status, and because of the era, we could call the doctor and he'd make a house call. He'd check us out, and then he'd prescribe. "Okay, go buy this medicine." Louisine was good for that, and I truly thank her. Not only did she report the bad things we did, but she was conscious of our health and made sure we ate properly. And that we ate together.

I grew up in a family of ten brothers and sisters, and even today, I guarantee you, if my brother would cook a meal, he would not eat until the rest of us arrived at his house. That's what really gives food that extra good taste—you're talking, you're sharing, you're enjoying some good wine with your great food. I've yet to meet a great chef who believes that eating alone is a good thing. Eating is something done as a couple, or in larger groups.

In my family, on many occasions, the topic around the table would be food. We would say, "Hey, last night, I think it was much better." Or, "You remember last time when you used a little more black pepper?" Or, "Today, I think you stressed the lime more." And this is something you're going to come across in the Haïtian cuisine, this question of memory and recollection, because we do not measure and record things. As a matter of fact, people who work with me in my restaurant's kitchen think they have a problem. They'll often ask me, "How many teaspoons?" No! I want you to look at what you're preparing, I want you to develop a feel for that particular piece of meat. I want you to naturally determine how many cups to add, how many spoonfuls, to get that perfect flavor for this particular moment in time, this particular cut of meat, this particular meal.

Measurements in Haïtian cuisine? That's almost a nonexistent thing. My brother Richard came to America at a very young age—I think he was probably like five or six years old—so he's probably the most "American" of our generation. Richard always gets on my case, asking me for recipe measurements. My reply is, "If I really want to be an authentic Haïtian, then measurements will never be in my kitchen!"

The only place you'll see measurement is if we are making cake or pastries. Desserts are delicate. If you're going to put yeast in a certain kind of batter, you cannot put too much in, or you'll spoil the batch. At my mother's bakery, she wouldn't use measurements when dividing up the wholesale selections into retail. But she would use them when making sweets. The flour she'd sell to customers at the general store, it'd arrive in fifty-pound sacks. She'd then divide them into saleable units, whatever size seemed right.

I learned to bake by watching my mother make bread, she and this guy who worked for her. They'd prepare baguettes and other breads on a large scale. The recipe would have been something like take fifty pounds of flour, add one gallon of shortening, one pound of salt, five tablespoons of yeast, and five gallons of water.

Making bread was important for my mother. After she left school, even trained as a nurse, there weren't many other kinds of work for her to do. So she started selling, using someone else's kitchen to start baking bread. At some point, her business grew big enough that she had to build her own bakery. This was on the same property as our house. I just called it a "house," but really, we're talking then about a three-room hut, with the five of us kids who were born at that point all sleeping in the same room. The hut was constructed with straw mixed with drywall. The straw was made up of grass, palm fronds, banana leaves, and other rots. Electricity? Definitely not. My mother to this day still spends part of her year in that hut, when she's not in Freeport, Long Island, residing in the six-bedroom house she purchased in the mid-seventies and that we all struggled for many years to pay [for]. It was the American Dream! A big white house in the suburbs! But when mom isn't living there, she's back in Haïti, in the hut. That's even though the family moved more than fifty years ago a quarter of a block away, to a far more solidly built house made by my uncle Melcourt. He was studying architecture at the time, and for his thesis project, he crafted this new house from stone and rock and cement. It was the best-built edifice in the area. We still own that house, plus the hut with the bakery attached.

Prior to our moving down the block into the stone house, the hut's kitchen would double as the place we'd cook our family meals as well as the kitchen for the bakery. The bakery didn't have any formal name, but everyone in town knew it as "Madame Georges." The bakery looked like it was sturdily built, but it wasn't. Constructing the bakery almost killed my uncle Abner. My mother was in a hurry to bake more bread. She couldn't wait for the concrete and dirt wall being built to cure. She convinced Abner, her younger brother, to go do some work before the mixture settled. The wall crashed down on Abner. He was buried for half an hour. Some people thought he wouldn't make it, but Abner was eighteen years old and a very strong man who used to lift weights. That strength really saved his neck.

Mom's bakery was the only one in town, and so people from all over would come to buy bread— especially during the Christmas season. This was the busiest time for mom. From November through mid-January, our family would be preoccupied baking bread. It was unbelievable. Everyone was involved. You couldn't excuse yourself—there was no choice, the work was happening right there inside the house. We could work the counter, interacting with customers, or we could help with the baking. I liked almost everything we made, but the public's favorite was clearly a bread the French call *canoe*, or "boat bread."

Let me tell you: year-round, people would come to the bakery—our house—and eat breakfast. They'd have juice and a canoe. Maybe some jelly or margarine or butter or peanut butter. At lunchtime, we'd sometimes offer sandwiches. Oh, that's another item my mother was good at: bread, salami, and cheese sandwiches, with pikliz on top. Pikliz, you'll read more soon, is like coleslaw.

So year-round was busy, but Christmas was the rush. Mom would make this special seasonal bread. I don't remember what she named it, but I remember it being shaped so it came to a point. We'd have to roll the dough a certain way and fold it. It was similar to a croissant. But it was a very basic bread, it didn't require any shortening, so it was very cheap for my mother to make. We would put a little bit of butter in it, butter that was made in Haïti. People would come in droves for that bread. So much so that I remember my mother never having the time to count the money coming in, because business would be so busy for that one period of time each year.

Yes, she never had time to properly, hygienically count the money. And guess what? I paid a very expensive price for that.

Right after I was born, I developed tetanus. That happened because my mother would sell, would count the money, and this one day she forgot to wash her hands and then went to clean my umbilical cord.

And guess what? Because of the bacteria that existed in that environment, I got sick. Tetanus. And really, the doctor thought that I was not going to make it, that I was not going to survive.

The doctor and the midwife and Louisine and my family, everyone rushed me to the hospital. When we arrived, the doctors were saying, "Hey, we gonna have to give him the last sacrament."

I had to be baptized at the hospital because they didn't think I was going to make it. They gave me injections left and right. And with the very last injection, the doctors said, "Mrs. Laguerre, we don't have any more spots on his body to inject any more medicine."

So my mother said, "I am going to try. I am going to give him that last injection."

You want to know something? It was that last injection that cured me. I'm alive today thanks to my mother's decision.

There was a side effect—I wasn't able for years to properly walk. Because where my mother gave me the injection to save my life, it also damaged some of the nerves on my left leg. So, one side of my body grew slightly bigger than the other.

We had a neighbor, a very nice old lady. She loved me as a kid. I was unable to walk properly, and she would give me therapy, every day, every morning, every afternoon. I would be playing, and she'd send for me. I used to hate it! You know, here you are five or six years old, you're playing, and this lady is calling you, "Hey, come over here, you gotta come here for your massage."

She gave me massages twice a day until I recovered at the age of eight. I was able to walk straight. It was almost like magic. And remember—this happened in the early sixties in a poor country. Really for me to even be alive today, I'm a blessed man.

But guess what—my surviving led to one oddity. I received baptism in the hospital, because no one thought I was going to survive. Everyone in the room wanted to make sure to honor different people, so everyone gave me a part of what became my very long name.

I was baptized by the head doctor of the hospital, who gave me a name. And then the head nurse of the hospital gave me a name. My father gave me a name. My mother gave me a name. Everyone in that room gave me a name! That's how I ended up with the moniker Jean-Marie Monfort Hébert Georges Fils Laguerre.

Years later, when I was ready to come to America, I presented my birth certificate to the consul. The consul said, "Wait a minute, in America we don't have that many names." He said, "Pick a first, middle, and last." I said, "Why don't you put, 'Georges Hébert Laguerre.'"

Many people here in Los Angeles know me as "Georges." Others back in Haïti as well as here at the restaurant call me "TiGeorges"—which means "Son of Georges"—my dad was named Georges. And "Fils" means "Junior," by the way. TiGeorges isn't part of my given name, but my dad did write it in, with his own handwriting, on the birth certificate.

I'm known by a few other names, too. My grandmother always called me "Zo," which means "bone" in French—as in "skinny as a bone." And a friend who lived next door to me in Port-de-Paix, she would call me "Monfo." "Hey, Monfo!" she'd say. Trust me, she wasn't saying that I was a "mofo"—a motherfucker! She just liked to sort of bastardize Monfort into "Monfo."

I'm most proud of the fact that my mother recently began to call me "Georges" without the "Ti" diminutive in front. I think she's proud of me, or it's a show of respect. Maybe in her mind, TiGeorges associates with little, it means small. And now she's looking at me as a big man, an achiever, and Georges is the most appropriate name to call me.

So yes, my mother. She ran that bakery. And the coins she handled every day almost killed me. And here I am, all these years later, running my own food establishment, handling food and handling currency. A friend of mine, he once asked me, "Are you tempting fate?"

You want to know something? I am so clean in my kitchen, it's unbelievable. I'll gladly take customers into my kitchen. When I first started the restaurant, I had such a great pride that I owned the place, I wanted to show the world. But because I'm from Haïti, people had doubts. "What does the kitchen look like? How does he handle the food?" They must think of Haïti as being an underdeveloped nation, so how could we know about cleanliness? Well, understand this: great cuisine comes with a clean kitchen. You cannot do good food and have a kitchen that is not up to code. Someone who enjoys cooking knows good food and good practices— for instance, you would never have raw meat next to something that has been cooked. That is a *no-no* in the kitchen. You cannot handle raw meat and then cooked food, especially chicken, which carries salmonella. In my kitchen, when I'm handling raw chicken, there's no other cooking that takes place, period. You have to be truly, truly very meticulous. And then there's something else related to cleanliness: presentation. I need to make certain that whatever I'm serving not only comes from a clean kitchen, but also delivers that vision of cleanliness to customers. I look at the plates, I inspect the food. I don't simply throw the meals out to you, thinking you're not going to notice or care what the stuff looks like! I'm sure people are going to see that someone who enjoys good food is gonna pay attention to every item on the plate. And they should. I know as well as anyone: poor health practices are no joke. I'm alive, but I almost never made it past that very first day of life.

CHICKEN

WHEN IT COMES TO the cuisine of Haïti, the poor can cook as well as the rich. When it comes to quality of food, you can go the bottom of the economic barrel of Haïti, and you will come across great quality of cuisine.

The poor have a different approach than the rich. The rich usually take a European standard approach. But when it comes to taste, the traditional Haïtian flavors are hard to beat.

In Haïti, was I rich or was I poor? Me, I was in the middle.

Yes, in the middle, definitely. What I've presented in this book are things that you come across in the middle class of Haïti. The food would be well-presented and well-balanced. Because in the middle you are well educated, you're in position to know about health factors—what is good for you and what you shouldn't eat.

My own foundation, my own upbringing and experiences, include relationships with both poor and rich. My grandmother couldn't read or write. But she was someone who really saw the future and made sure that we knew about a better tomorrow. She truly made the path for us. So now let me shine some light on that path as it led up to opening of TiGeorges' Chicken.

I'd come to Los Angeles to try and take advantage of my undergraduate film school education—I'd gone to the School of Visual Arts (SVA) back in New York. But I didn't have the connections or the demeanor to make it in Hollywood. I did odd jobs instead—boating, banking, even a perhaps-foreshadowing turn at a horrible fast food chicken joint. All the while, though, I was thinking up entrepreneurial enterprises. One of the ideas I launched with my now ex-wife. A party supplies rental business. We not talking balloons and clowns here, we talking tents and awnings and tables and chairs and heat lamps and cutlery and crockery and the like. If you've seen TiGeorges' Chicken grow over the years, you've most likely seen the party supply business too. For years, until the restaurant expanded in 2008, the party business was located in the storefront next door, here on Glendale Boulevard in Echo Park.

I had a side business back then, too. Freight forwarding. It was a very interesting operation—you deliver loads quickly to places that larger couriers and delivery services can't get through immediately. I know, I know—sounds like some smuggling operation. But no, it was quite a legitimate business. "Go to San Pedro, to the port, get this load. Go to LAX, the airport, get this load." I never would have known about this delivery niche, except that my cousin worked for a freight forwarding operation. And I started doing a little work for him when he needed help.

One day my cousin called and said, "Come pick up a load." I said okay and went to the harbor. I met up with my cousin and it turned out that his boss was having the same kinds of problems as me: personal problems, marital problems. So apparently his boss was going to lose the business. I said to my cousin, "Well, you're going to lose your job." He said, "Yeah, I am." So I said, "Why don't you come and try to do the freight forwarding for me?" He said, "Yeah, I can do that."

So my cousin came with me. We were doing the work and everything was groovy. We had one account. This Japanese guy. We were moving freights and *samovars* to Hawaii and the Mariana Islands. It was fun, but the money was no good and I didn't want to spend my life becoming a long-hauler. I figured, "Okay, time to do something I care about." Something I've dreamed about. Something my family might say I was raised to do—get the restaurant going.

At the party supplies business, I worked with an interesting and smart woman named Claudia. I said, "Claudia, we've got to find a place with a barbeque grill for sale." Oh man, she and I called all over the country. We called Chicago. We called Tennessee. Any state I associated with barbecuing and rotisserie chicken, we called. The grills we located at first were all gas operated. I said no. I wanted my food to carry that wood-burned flavor, that Haïtian flavor. I planned to marinate the birds the way we did in Haïti and cook them on a spit with a fire fed from aromatic logs. This was a specific idea—not just any ol' grill would do.

☼ ☼ ☼

EVENTUALLY, I CAME ACROSS a guy in Texas—very interesting guy. I think he was Italian. I told him the idea. He said, "Georges, I don't have anything. No no no, Georges." We kept talking, though, and then after a while he said, "You know, I think we have something that we can convert."

"Okay, what is it?" I said. And I asked him how big the grill—the spit—was. "How many rows are there for the chickens?" I asked. He answered, "Well, there are three arms on the spit and each of 'em can fit five chickens at once. But I can it redesign it, Georges, and make 'em each take six." That would mean I'd be able to cook somewhere in the neighborhood of eighteen chickens at a time. Six on each arm of the rotisserie. I said, "Great, wonderful!"

Then he said to me, "The machine costs about six thousand five hundred dollars." I said, "Wow, that's a lot of money." And then I said, "I'm going to make this work."

I had an Iveco truck—an Italian truck, right? Let me tell you: I was in love with that truck. It was like the Italians say, raw *gusto*! It was a big truck in a small frame. Let me tell you: I could pick up all kinds of crazy loads with that truck. But when it broke down, it was expensive to repair. So I decided to sell the truck. I put an ad in the *Recycler* newspaper. This guy calls me and says, "Yes, I will buy the truck." I told him I wanted six thousand dollars. He said, "Nah, the best I can give you is four thousand dollars."

I said, "Oh man, no, that won't be enough." I told him that four thousand five hundred dollars is the best I could do. He said okay. So the guy gave me four thousand five hundred dollars cold cash money. So I called the barbeque grill company to let them know, "Hey guess what? I have some money. Are you able to sell me this barbeque grill for four thousand five hundred dollars?"

The guy said, "Georges, you gotta be crazy. You gotta be insane. No I can't do that, Georges."

I said, "I'm going to send you four thousand five hundred dollars right now. That's all I have."

He said, "Georges *Georges Georges* you can't do that!" Let me tell you: I must have worn that man down. After a long back-and-forth, he said, "All right, Georges. You should give me that four thousand five hundred dollars. I'm not going to be able to give you that barbeque grill right now. You're going to have to wait for it." That was fine with me. I went ahead and bought a money order for four thousand five hundred dollars and sent it via FedEx. The following day I called to find out if he had received the money. He said yes.

I waited six months for that barbeque grill. Six months! Then the guy said, "Georges, the barbeque grill is ready. It's on its way." *Wow.* What do I do now? I didn't have the freight money. All I could think was, "Let me call my brother Richard."

"Hey, Richard," I said. "I got this idea. I wanna open up a restaurant. I'm gonna do this, I'm gonna do that. What do you think?" I told him I was asking him because I needed money right then to receive the centerpiece, the grill. Richard said, "I'm going to give you five hundred dollars for the freight." God, thank God! So Richard gave me the five hundred dollars.

During this same period, I was moving the party supplies store, and acquiring the space for what would soon become the restaurant location. And guess what? It wasn't my first choice for a location.

This real estate guy that I knew—of course, an Italian again. I guess I'm very lucky with Italians, always have been. My brother Taylor, remember, when he was in college he was studying Italian, and he speaks it very well. My cousin Norman speaks Italian. And when we were kids, my mother used to sell Italian products at her store, from olive oil, you name it, to salami, to cheese. But anyway, the real estate agent said to me, "Georges, I have a place." But I was used to being in a big warehouse, out of the public eye, where the rent was really cheap. He said, "Georges, I got a place that used to be a restaurant before. And I can get you that place no problem." And the agent said, "I need eighteen hundred dollars for the deposit for the monthly rent."

The guy took me to see the place. It looked okay. I was in a hurry because I was being forced to move out from the old place, the warehouse. The owner there, he originally wanted to sell me that building. Actually, he wanted to give it to me. But because I wasn't sure— my marriage wasn't going well and I didn't feel secure enough to responsibly take on the note of a property that was a half-block long. It was too bad—the guy was basically going to hand it to me. "Georges, you give me ten thousand dollars, you pick up the note," he'd said. "I will give you the note and I will transfer the title into your name."

My not taking the deal apparently pissed the guy off. And then this guy from Thailand came into the complex and started doing garment work. Fast-moving guy, sharp, sneaky—there was always a problem with him. "Hey, Georges, move your truck! Oh, Georges, move this! Oh, Georges!" So this guy was getting on my nerves, pushing me around, pushing me there. So he went to see the property manager, telling the manager that he wanted to expand his garment outfit.

Well, I don't know what the manager said in reply, but one thing I know is that when I paid the guy, he would keep the check, not deposit it. *Ohhhhhh.* I kept saying to myself, "How come I have that kind of money?" So the guy didn't cash the check for three months, meaning he was going to build a case on me to evict me: "Oh, so you don't pay, you gotta get out." When I discovered that he wasn't cashing the check I redrew the money, got a cashiers check, and brought it to the manager. So when the guy realized that he could not kick me out that way, he came and said all straightforward, "You know something, Georges, we need the property. I'm going to need you to move."

So I moved where the real estate agent suggested. And when I got there, I found out there was no place to park the truck. There was a big tree in front of the place, obscuring the storefront. And worst of all, the realtor had claimed that there had been a restaurant in the space previously, and that all the equipment remained. There was no equipment. Here I was wanting to start a restaurant. In my mind there was going to be an oven hood, a kitchen, everything was going to be in order, all I'm going to do is install my custom grill once it arrives from Texas. Then I'd get inspected, and I'm in business. Oh no. It wasn't so. Once I figured out how much money it was going to cost to acquire everything else I needed, I had to put the restaurant on hold again.

So I waited. And whenever I could afford to, I'd purchase a piece of equipment. Every time the party rentals business made a little money, I'd buy something for the restaurant. It took four years to afford everything I needed. I wasn't taking home any profit from the party business. I couldn't afford to pay all my bills. So I sold my house at no profit, and started renting in Mount Washington.

I told you, though, us Haïtians, we are relentless! And we are fraternal. There was a guy, a very dear friend named Laurent who loved me very much. That love first came from his dad. As kids, we were thrilled to receive candy from our parents and neighbors. My mom had candy at her store, of course—we were fortunate, we had everything. But guess what? The candies that Laurent's dad used to give me—they tasted better. Every afternoon I would stand at the intersection between my family's house and Laurent's. I would wait for his dad to make his turn, so I could then receive a candy from him.

I cherished that candy! And on occasion, Laurent's dad would even give me a couple of gourdes. So now, here I am, a lifelong friend of this man's son. Laurent is a doctor, he really grew up right. Everyone knows Laurent. He and Walner, who is over at NASA, we all grew up together. Those two, I'm so proud of both of them. They've accomplished so much in America.

So Laurent, I gave him a call. I whispered to him, "I've got an idea, you know. I want to build a restaurant."

I described the vision. He was supportive. And he and his wife decided to come out west for a visit. This meant so much to me! I said to Laurent, "I'm going to surprise you."

How? By turning my backyard into a blueprint of what the restaurant would be. I'd already built that roto prototype. I cooked the chicken that day exactly as I wanted it to be. I set a table with chairs, china, all the glassware, all very nice. I added a candle. I even put a small piece of wood, a small log, as the table's centerpiece, to symbolize I was going to do wood-burned rotisserie chicken. Laurent came, and his wife. You know, it had to be love. For him to fly from Baltimore. For him to come and spend time and even sleep at my house! So that was a great thing. I think that gave me all the energy that I needed to make this thing go forward. And we ate, and he and his wife loved the meal. Then I said to Laurent, "Would you like to become an investor?"

He didn't say anything. He didn't say no. He said, "Okay, alright, cool." So I left it at that, ambiguous. Then Laurent said, "If you're going to do this, it's got to be a corporation. You should make a corporation." Yes, okay! He asked if I knew how. I said I'd find out.

Well, okay, I did the research. "Well, Georges, this and that. You should incorporate here, you should incorporate there." I found a company on the Internet. Next, I needed to calculate shares. I had to estimate, "How much money am I going to make?" I determined,

"Well, it's going to cost at least thirty thousand dollars." Laurent said, "Why don't you put this on paper?"

I'm an artist. I'm a filmmaker. That's what I went to school for. I was good at visualizing the thing, what it's going to cost, how it's going to be set up, how best to sell the chicken. I said to Laurent, "I could sell you twenty percent." He said, "Okay, how much?" I settled on twelve thousand five hundred dollars. That would be his share. He said, "Yes, good." Then my brother talked to me and I asked him, "Do you want to buy action?" He said, "Yeah, sure." Then I called my sister Mary. "You want action?" "Yeah, sure!" My cousin Norma? "Yeah, sure!" My cousin Ketty. "Yeah, sure!" Everybody said yes, no questions asked. It felt wonderful. Then I thought, "Why don't I give some stock to my sister Danielle?" She never gave me any money, but she's my sister and I wanted her to be a part of it. Then I realized, "Well, I'm going to have a corporation, and the corporation doesn't have an accountant. Where can I find an accountant?" When things really get juicy, we start making big money, we're going to need somebody to keep the score, to really check. I thought of Sosthenes, my good buddy. Sosthenes is an expert in that department. I said, "Sosthenes I'd like you to be part of this corporation." He didn't say anything except for, "No problem." Well, since he's part of the corporation, I gave him some stock. Then my cousin Alfred, who always helping me this way and that. "*Ahh,* you helped me build it, I'll give you some stock."

Then Gabriel, of course. He and I are always hanging around. Gabriel, he's always telling me the restaurant is not clean enough. "Oh, Georges, why don't you change your outfit or your appearance? Oh, Georges." But he's not going to wash a plate. Gabriel wash a plate? Gabriel pick up a chair? Oh no. Gabriel always wears white gloves, trust me. But he knows his stuff. I thought, "Okay, we need his acumen, I'm going to give him some action." He said, "I have a freezer. I will give a freezer for the stock."

Okay, good! He wanted to be part, too. So now I'm getting closer—I'm truly going to be able to open up a restaurant and it's wood-burning, right? We're going to cook chicken on an open wood fire and people are going to see the chicken dripping fat, the flames rising, and so forth, and people are going to walk by the scores into the restaurant and buy chicken.

Well, my estimate of thirty-two thousand dollars in start-up costs turned into seventy thousand dollars. Having to buy all that equipment. Having to have a hood and vent system custom built in order to satisfy the health department and the fire department. But everything was paid with cash. I didn't borrow money from the bank to build TiGeorges' Chicken. I didn't realize until years later that building up TiGeorges' Chicken in cash was the best thing that I could ever have done. Because, you know, most restaurants fail during the very first six months. What's the percentage?

I think they say it's ninety percent. So all these years I'm still in business. And without bank debts.

That doesn't mean I've been flush. I passed the health inspection. And then here I was, opening up the restaurant! I climbed up on a short ladder and spelled out, "Grand Opening!" on my marquee. My assumption was that people were gonna take one look through the big windows at the birds cooking, and they'd all come right in. *Sheesh*, it didn't happen.

I was scrambling to pay my earliest bills. Since those first days, I've been buying chickens from Cisco, the supplier. Cisco has a five-hundred-dollar minimum order. Why do I use them? Before I opened, every place I went, I asked, "Where can you buy chicken?" Nobody would tell me. I couldn't believe this. Every supermarket has chicken. Almost every restaurant has chicken on their tables everyday. Everybody knows who sells chicken in large quantity. But nobody was going to tell me—maybe they feared more competition? It doesn't make sense. I wound up calling Tyson in Arkansas. The Tyson guy said, "You should call Cisco." So, I had to spend five bills. That's a lotta chicken for a brand-new small business.

The first Cisco delivery arrived the same day I was having my cash register programmed. I knew Cisco was due, so I left a check for the driver. While I was out in a different part of Los Angeles, I received a call. "Oh, guess what," I was told, "Cisco won't take a check, the driver wants cash because you're a first-time customer." Holy cow. What am I going to do? Here I am somewhere way out in the San Fernando Valley. "Tell him to wait for me, I'm coming," I said. So I'm rushing back, and guess what? A motorcycle cop has staged himself at a traffic intersection. He's staged himself cleverly, so it looks like he's parked outside a business, like he's inside getting coffee or a cruller. I drove by, going about fifty miles per hour in a thirty-five zone, and I knew I was busted. The guy was standing near his bike, holding a radar gun in his hands. He motioned for me to pull over, he ticketed me. So I paid a guy fifty dollars to reprogram three line items on the cash register, and then I got a 145-dollar ticket, and I was holding up my chicken supplier even longer.

When I got back to Glendale Boulevard though, let me tell you: I forgot those money troubles! Wow. There was a forty-eight-footer parked in front of my restaurant. Everybody in the neighborhood was out looking, saying, "Check Georges out, with his restaurant, with this big truck coming." Oh, I felt like an important man. I was really excited.

So, the register is working. The marquee text is up. My signage is up. And my five hundred dollars worth of chickens are in the cooler. I lit the wood, put a single bird on the rotisserie, and started cooking.

The place looked so good. The place smelled so good. This is the American Dream!

Except nobody came to eat. Nobody came in that first day to buy a meal from TiGeorges' Chicken.

The second day, I sold one plate. One. Plate. *Uh-oh.* I'm thinking, *Shit. This is not going to work.* All these people I'm watching across the street, they're going into the Thai place to buy teriyaki chicken. All I can think is, "In New York, they'd cross the street. People are curious. I guess people in California are very different."

I'm embarrassed to admit that, but that's what I was thinking—can you imagine? Blaming the potential customers? Let me tell you: I was stressed out. I got to thinking, *What can I do?* Well, since I had on hand all these tables and chairs from the party supplies business next door, I decided to do some marketing. I made a sort of patio out front—I set up a table, two chairs, and a shade umbrella. I put a white tablecloth out, with some fresh flowers and my nicest silverware and glassware.

So now, guess what? I went inside for just a moment and by the time I'd come back out, one of the chairs was gone. Someone stole it. I said, "Well, that ain't gonna stop me!" I put out a new chair. And I waited. Well, that table worked. People hadn't seen a place to eat in this location for a long time, so they'd stopped looking. By the end of the week, though, slowly but surely, customers came. That positive motorcyclist. That negative neighbor. And executives from downtown—the bankers, the guys who work for the Los Angeles Department of Water and Power, the Los Angeles Unified School District. All these people with offices located pretty much nearby. It was more than a relief. This saved my business when it was at its most vulnerable.

Soon, customers were asking: "How do you do the grill?" I'd say, "Well you know, sometimes I cook the chicken with avocado wood, or with citrus on occasion, like orange." They'd say things like, "Really? Tastes good." So people would eat and eat and all was going fine but not gangbusters. Then, guess what? A month later, someone reviewed me in the *Los Angeles Times*. "The wood-burning pit, the savory, smoky avocado flavor. The Haïtian chicken. It's a must try. TiGeorges' has the greatest chicken in the West." Or, it was something positive like that. Significantly, the writer said I used avocado wood, and didn't mention any of the other kinds. I thought, "*Whoa*, since that's in print, I better find more avocado wood. I better use avocado wood all the time. Otherwise people are going to come in and be upset, challenge me, not believe me."

Getting that avocado wood for the rotisserie became an obsession. And it went from being almost a comical exploration of the city's forgotten alleyways to a weekly road trip to a place of great beauty.

Originally, I was buying my wood from this professional tree-trimmer up in the Lancaster area. He had this big open field where he'd dump all the wood he'd collect while doing his jobs. Gabriel, my friend, was living out there and told me I should go to Highway 14, to whatever exit, and I'd see the wood off to my right. So I did. And I started buying. The seventy dollar cost per week was plenty for a restaurant that wasn't bringing in much scratch. It was a long ride, too, and hard work filling up the truck with logs, then bringing them back and unloading and stacking them. The work was unavoidable. But what about the money? I thought, *I've got to find a way to cut down the amount.* So I started searching the back alleys of LA, seeking out wood that had been trashed. You know how people who don't have much money don't want to go pay a fee to dispose trash? They'll just put the goods in their alley. I'd see all sorts of stuff—auto body parts, a barber's chair, piles of clothing. Every Sunday, that's what I'd do—drive the back alleys of okay, bad, and worse neighborhoods, on an avocado wood quest. No pine—that's not good for cooking. No rubber trees. No succulents. No palms. I was cruising behind Alvarado Street here in Echo Park, when I spied a tremendous tree. It turned out to have been chopped down the night before. I stopped my van and knocked on the door closest to the tree. I asked the guy who answered if I could take the tree. "Yeah, wonderful," he said.

I cut that tree by hand with an old hacksaw. Hard work. I said to myself, "This tree will be perfect for a week. I've got to do something." I went to Home Depot and bought a chain saw. I started cutting. But guess what? It was difficult. The chain lost its sharpness quickly. You know how people who have trees in their backyards drive nails in them to hang clothing lines and hammocks or who knows what else—archery targets? Proclamations? Well, if you nail a young tree, that tree will grow over that entry point and you'll lose sight of the nail. So it's a great surprise when your chainsaw breaks because it's hit a nail. *Ahh*, there were so many nails. I only could cut enough wood for two days. Perhaps city alley trees weren't the panacea I'd anticipated.

The next week, something popped into my head. I used to go play bingo up near Santa Barbara in this little town somewhere in the Santa Ynez area. I remember seeing this avocado plantation with big piles of timber. The way the piles were staggered, it was like an invitation. "If you want some, come and get some." But that had been a few years prior. I went up the next Sunday to try and find the spot again, and see what was going on. I got lost, I drove all around, I didn't know if I was heading east or west or over to Cuba or the Dominican or maybe Goleta. Finally, I passed in front of a little place that had just chopped down a bunch of eucalyptus trees.

I was seeking avocado but I figured maybe the guys here will know something. I pulled in and said to the first guy I met, "How you doing?" This turned out to be the foreman. A really nice guy. We spoke in Spanish. He said, "Those eucalyptus trees, we already promised them to another guy." That guy was letting the trees dry out some more, he was due in later that week to pick them up. But the foreman said to me—it was unbelievable what he said. "We've got something else," he said. "We've got forty acres of avocado trees. All those over there. We want to give them to you. Bring your truck around."

I couldn't believe it! That Sunday, boy did I ever load up the truck. Of course, I had a girlfriend with me, and her daughter. The daughter said to me, "Georges, you hit bingo. You struck gold." And she was right. Santa Ynez bingo was never this good. Even a young kid could see how great this was. My problem was solved. My supply was set. Everybody in LA could go on talking about my avocado wood–burned chicken.

I got better cooking with the stuff. Avocado wood burns intensely. It goes up quickly. So you have the tendency to cook the chicken too fast—the outside cooks first, the inside not so well. This means you have to monitor the chicken more, turn it more, prod it more. It's more labor-intensive than working with other woods. Let me tell you: it's worth it! The flavor is incredible.

Every couple of Sundays I'd drive north to collect more wood. It seemed too good to be true, so superstitiously, I kept thinking, "I don't want the owner of the property to see me. He might change his mind. He might not even know what I'm doing." I'd only deal with the foreman, and I'd only go early in the morning, when I figured the big boss would be sleeping or maybe at church or at brunch with his family. Each time I'd say to the foreman, "How are you? How's everything?" I'd offer him money for the wood, too. Mostly as a courtesy, because every time he'd say no. "The boss already pays me," he'd say.

One Saturday, it rained. That's a rare event in this desert climate. So I waited until Sunday afternoon to go north, to give the wood a chance to dry. Next thing I know, I see a big old Volkswagen coming my way, driving fast. I said, "Oh shit, this has got to be the owner." Then he parked. A white guy. He came over and said, "How you doing, Mister? It's Georges, right? Hey, I'm Bill."

I said, "I'm the guy you said could take the wood." He said, "Yeah, it's okay. Yeah, of course." Then he said, "Where would you like me to leave the wood for you? And what dimensions you want me to cut them for you? Tell me, because the guy who's cutting can trim that stuff to any dimension." Things got even better. Bill said, "Follow me, there's this place on the other side where we have more wood—you can take it all." Then the guy showed me the whole property. He said, "Over here, it's yours." So now I've got wood through the nose. Thank you, Bill.

I'm really truly a blessed man to discover the avocado for free. And above all to learn how to use the avocado wood because it's not something that's in the culture of America. America doesn't use avocado wood. But in Haïti, we burn all kinds of wood, because wood's what we use for solid fuel. We make coal out of it. And we burn it to cook. Anyway, thank God that I had found avocado wood because after people had read in the newspaper that that's all I used, I knew at some point someone was going to come by and confirm this to be true. So in back of the counter, near the rotisserie, I would rack 'em up, load it up with avocado wood, you know? And then indeed, one day, there was this lady who came in and said to me, "Is it true that you use avocado wood?" And I said, "Yes, of course, I use avocado wood! Come on back, come over here." I took her behind the counter to show her, and I told her how I'd travel to pick up the wood.

She said, "I'll be damned. I paid a man five hundred dollars last month to clear my backyard. I had a tree that I had cut many years ago and it was really in the way. Oh man, damn, I could have saved money and you could have saved a trip to Santa Barbara." So, yeah, people were paying attention. Newspapers aren't dead yet! And for me, both gambling—playing bingo—and hard work—trolling alleys and exurbias—paid off. So did my following up. You can tell me "no" if you want, but I'll find a way to get things done.

After all, starting TiGeorges' Chicken was nothing if not a delusion. I thought that once I opened my door—because of the grill, the fire, the chicken, cooking in front of everyone—the food was going to be sold out immediately. Remember that second day I told you about? I was with my two guys, my sons, Benjamin and Michael, and we only sold one plate of food. Seven dollars and thirty-one cents. To this guy by the name of Matt. Matt worked for UPS and he started coming every day for lunch. But that day, he was all alone. Michael said, "Dad, we only sold seven dollars and thirty-one cents today. You think we're going to make it?" That was really rough.

Then the business people started coming. The *Times*. *Los Angeles Downtown News* gave me a review. Hey, very interesting! That newspaper came out on a Sunday. On a Monday, December 16, I'll never forget what happened. Huell Howser called TiGeorges'. I couldn't believe it. Huell Howser! I said to him, "Are you sure you're Huell Howser?" He said, "Yes, TiGeorges, I'm Huell Howser." I said, "No, it can't be!" He said, "TiGeorges, when do you think I can come to your restaurant to shoot a documentary about you and your goat?"

Well, I said, "Huell, usually Wednesday is my slowest day."

I was making seven dollars and thirty-one cents. Every day was a slow day for me, okay?

Huell Howser said, "Wednesday, what about to-morrow?"

I thought, "Oh damn, Huell Howser is coming!" I said yes. I went ahead and shaved. Got a haircut. Made myself look good. Prepared everything. And then Huell Howser came, and let me tell you: that was a dream come true.

Here I am, a guy who went to film school, who always wanted to be the cameraman. Now, me and my restaurant are in front of the camera for a full half-hour, and on what was then Los Angeles' PBS affiliate. Let me tell you: that's when the big break came through.

And I must say, if it wasn't for Huell Howser, TiGeorges' Chicken probably wouldn't be in existence today.

I remember Huell Howser saying, "TiGeorges, I'm going to do something that I've never done before in my life: I'm going to air the show back-to-back. Are you ready?" I said, "Huell, I am ready."

He said, "TiGeorges, are you sure you're ready?"

"I said, yes, I'm ready." But you want to know something? I was not ready!

Because people came by the dozens. I mean, we're talking about two months, three months with a consistent flow of people coming in to enjoy TiGeorges' Chicken. People are devoted to Huell Howser's television show! And you want to know something? I learned something very interesting during this process: how to pre-prepare things, how to kind of stage a situation. From that point forward, TiGeorges' Chicken was really ready. Thank you again, Huell, and may you rest in peace. Like so many other fans of you and your work, my family and I were saddened by your passing in 2013.

RED SNAPPER

MY DAD DIDN'T LIKE America.

The guy, you could tell he was in pain. Because he had to perform certain tasks, he had to learn to fix himself a sandwich. Whereas in Haïti, it was, "Oh, he's hungry?" He'd be asked, "Oh, what would you like?" And then somebody would bring that dish to him.

Haïti is a country with so many poor people. That means a man with money can afford to hire help. But again, there's also that attitude that permeates—the guy who has no money but receives an education and then feels entitled, like, "The maid has to do it." No. You can do it yourself. I've gone back to Haïti and I try to help. Like with that lime project I started. I attempted to work with one cousin in particular. When I wasn't there, well, I expect him to realize, "This is for me, this is for Georges, and this is for my country. I'm part of something. I'm participating. I'm going to contribute." And instead I'd hear the guy go, "Oh, I'm in college." Or, "I'm gonna take my baccalaureate. I cannot dig a hole to plant a tree." He did next to nothing for an entire year. This is a problem.

Does this guy want to work? Heck no, he was a recent graduate and supposed to be working. But in his mind, he thinks, "Why would I do that sort of work?" Instead he'll call another guy without any education to dig the hole. This needs to be corrected—people who won't do the work. What percentages of Haïtians are like this? I don't know. Sixty percent? Higher, maybe. Seventy-five percent?

Another example: when we were kids, my brother Taylor took the hose and cleaned off the sidewalk. Guess what? A lady was passing by, and she couldn't believe what this well-dressed guy was doing. She said, "Oh, this has to be one of the sons of Germaine Poux-Laguerre," who, yes, is our mother. Because we were brought up to get stuff done. Whereas some other guys we knew, it was, "Hey, I'm an educated guy, I should be doing paperwork. I shouldn't get involved to anything physical." Well, fine, if you do indeed have an office job. But if you're unemployed? C'mon. I'm sure that here in

America, some rich guy, a guy who owns a ranch, who probably has millions of dollars, he'd climb into a tractor and go plow the soil. Does that make him a lesser man? And this guy probably went to Harvard or Cornell. And yet this is a task that needs to be performed. And if he's a guy who can handle a machine, then what does a diploma have to do with anything? Why in Haïti can't we celebrate hard work and self-reliance as universal values?

My family, we grew up in a nice stone house. We had a place to park the car. A backyard with mango trees that we used to go climb. That was our pastime. That and raising pigeons. Oh, man. We built cages for them. At some point, we had more than one hundred birds. Different colors. We would feed them corn. We didn't have any toys at home purchased from stores— we would make our own. We would take cardboard boxes and make trucks. We would build our own toy boats by splitting coconuts in half and adding a stick and some cloth for the mast. We'd run down to the beach and put the coconut boats in the ocean. If it was a really windy day, let me tell you: those boats would sail far and wide! Hey, who knows? Maybe all the way to Cuba. In Haïti, that's what we did at the beach. Make boats out of coconuts. Have picnics and eat lambi. Fly kites—that was popular. No one ever taught us how to swim, though. When I came to America, I said, "Oh, big swimming pools!" The lifeguard, he said, "Oh, I got to teach you how to swim."

In my country, we don't teach people how to swim. You don't know how to swim? Don't let another friend know that. Why? Because he'll wait for you to get near the ocean, or sit on a pier, and then he'll push you off. Let me tell you: within five minutes, you would become a swimmer! I mean, you better figure it out! Because you start swallowing water. Next thing you know, you find a way to swim to shore. That's how I was taught. This is something that you learn yourself. Once you're able to float, that's when you learn the backstroke, then you move into the butterfly. Then you're going to go diving, head in first. Or you can jump into the water.

During summertime, I probably spent more than half my days at the beach. I remember my grandmother saying, "Young boys don't stay in bed past 6:00 a.m." And so we brothers had to get up at that hour. What did we do? There was very little to do, so we would go fishing early in the morning. We'd usually get home in time for dinner. We'd be so interested in the fishing that sometimes we'd forget about eating. Our parents would then send a maid to get us. Whenever we'd see the maid coming, we'd say, "Oh shit, that means dinnertime!"

The sad thing about fishing was we had to drop them; we weren't supposed to take those fish home. Why not? Because we came from a business family. Fisherman is a low profession. As kids, all we ever heard was, "Oh, you're going to school? Especially a Catholic school? You have no business fishing."

When we were a little bit older, my brothers and I would reply, "We're going fishing. Period. We'll bring the catch home." The response to that? "Oh no, you shouldn't have to do that. The maid can do that." I'm almost certain that attitude still exists in Haïti. It's just not a good practice. My grandmother was an exception. If you were keeping busy, if you were occupied doing something—cooking or fishing or hosing off sidewalks or whatever—that was acceptable to my grandmother. She felt anything was constructive versus being out on the street, doing things that might get a kid in trouble. Very few people felt that same way. You're a doctor? So what? Just because you're a doctor doesn't mean you don't know how to sweep the floor of your house or how to boil an egg. Like in the kitchen, my dad couldn't boil an egg. But, oh boy, I do remember how much my dad loved that stuff—he loved his eggs sunny-side up. This is not really common in Haïtian cuisine. Everything is basically scrambled and usually mixed with shallot, with herring, and some other stuff. A Haïtian omelet, that's what it is. We only do omelets, we don't have sunny-side up or over easy. The only person I saw eating sunny-side up was my dad. And truly, I don't know where he learned that.

Why herring in a Haïtian omelet? You think that's only a Nordic cuisine? Don't underestimate the richness of Haïtian culture. When I was growing up, you'd find everything. You'd find the world. That's why in Haïti, when you see a meal prepared, don't be surprised to see something that came from Europe, something that came from America, something that came from Africa. And in Haïti, we truly love herring. It is one of the principle items on the menu. We cook herring with rice, with mushrooms. We basically put herring on everything. Lunch, breakfast, and dinner. We would mix up how we served it. We'd do dumplings. And of course, acra—tarot root—has herring in it. And we'd make fritay. The recipe for fritay is pretty much the same throughout Haïti. If we're not having fritay as a late-night street food snack, then we're having it before a meal, as an appetizer. We'll consume it with a biscuit. It is basically chopped onions with habanero chili, vinegar, and olive oil, and in this case, herring. All that mixed together. Let me tell you: you've got to pay attention to your fingers or you might end up biting them. That's how good that stuff is.

At TiGeorges', in the earliest days, halibut was the only fish I had on the menu. No, not halibut, I'm sorry! I used to have halibut, but it was too expensive for what my customers were looking to pay, and not considered exotic enough. I switched to red snapper, which is also a relatively expensive fish. But red snapper is more associated with a tropical environment. When you say, "Haïtian restaurant" and "red snapper," it strikes customers as something they'd encounter while in the Caribbean. And they are correct! In Haïti we enjoy red snapper many different ways. We can dry it. Okay? We can fry it. We can make stew out of it. But in my restaurant, I fry. It's faster to fry and more manageable because I can prepare a meal and freeze it and when somebody wants it, I can fry it and serve it within ten minutes. On the menu, my snapper comes with "Kreyol sauce Charlotte." What's in it? Oregano, which I put on all seafood. Sautéed garlic. Plenty of key lime juice. Black pepper. Habanero chili. Hey, if you enjoy tropical food, then you truly must enjoy habanero chili or Scotch bonnet chili.

My relationship with red snapper goes way back. As kids, fishing, we'd catch snapper and yellowtail. Just once, we caught *delaqet*. It's a special fish, a very small fish. You could never catch one. I remember one day, my friend Max hooked one! That was the story of the month. Oh man, this is a rare fish to catch, you know? You would bring your little bait. The delaqet would eat all the bait. You would stay there for *hours hours hours*, he would keep coming and *eating eating eating*. If you could catch one, then that would classify you as a real fisherman.

Another thing from my childhood: I remember going down to the river, too, not just the ocean. To catch crawfish at the river required some talent, some ingenuity. You gotta watch out for your fingers, because you don't want to get bitten. Usually that crawfish would be under a rock, so you'd have to move the rock in such a gentle way as to not disturb that crawfish. You don't want to surprise him, but yet, you have to surprise him, to your advantage. If you were able to catch five crawfish at the river, let me tell you: you were really considered a top kid in the neighborhood. Because you had an extra talent that other guys didn't have. You know, you could do well at *futból*, volleyball, playing cards, or be good in school. But catching that crawfish, that definitely, truly provided an edge.

When I talk about the river, I mean what we call *Trois Riviere*. It's three rivers merged into one. That river was always dirty. I understand why: erosion. Most of the roads nearby were not paved, and that's where the dirt would flow from. There's always rain in Haïti, especially during September. All the water from the city would dispose into the river. So you'd always see this dirty river, this muddy color, which then becomes bad for the ocean. Once that muddy water made it through the river and out to sea, it would diminish fishing.

Still, as kids, let me tell you: we couldn't wait for that rainy season! Why? Because we knew the river would flood the city and if we couldn't then walk to school, we'd get the day off. If it rained for a week, bodies of water would connect and then, like people say back in Brooklyn, *fugheddaboutit*! You might as well be homeschooled. Flooding was so common that it affected basic engineering practices—sidewalks located closer to the river would be three or four feet higher than sidewalks farther away.

Yeah, I'm talking here about crawfish and flooding and missing school. Yeah, I'm from the provinces. There's a tendency in Haïti among people from the capital to think, "Well, if he's from the province, he's less of a person." What difference does it make? Should I say the guy from Brooklyn is lesser than the guy from Manhattan, or the Bronx, or Queens? I attended Catholic school in Port-au-Prince. It was my first extended experience in the capital. And I thought, "Oh, man, this is something I'm going to hate." I was always called out as a "the guy from the provinces." So, I am provincial. Big deal. Hey, usually the guy from the province is the guy who has more intelligence. The guy who is willing to learn more. The guy who is more capable on all levels. But that guy from the capitol, maybe he has a fancy car, and he's able to buy a nice French-made shirt. Whereas the guy from the provinces would buy the local stuff or have homemade clothing. Haïti is such a small country. About two hundred kilometers. We're not talking about going across the world! To pretend to see such a big gap between Haïtian places—it's pathetic.

I'm saying this even though I had family in Port-au-Prince. My dad's sisters, my aunts, lived there, and I'd stay with her and my cousins. I much preferred going further southwest, though, to Bainet, where my father was from. Going to his hometown was great. People would love seeing us. They'd say, "Oh, are you the son of Georges?" People would do almost anything for us, because they had such respect for my dad. He was so well liked. I miss my dad, and I miss that place.

You know, looking back, I could make the case that there was no need for my family to emigrate to the United States. In Haïti, we had so much: a maid to wash, a maid to cook, a maid to clean, the respect of friends and neighbors, family throughout the country, good businesses. We had it all. But then my uncle Melcourt came here, and my mom came to visit him, and that was it. She decided to move.

Now, let me stress, I'm very happy for my sake, and for Benjamin and Michael's sake, that my mother came here. But in retrospect, I'm acknowledging, hey, it didn't have to happen. There were certain levels of comforts available in Haïti that the Laguerres haven't yet attained in the United States.

But hey, remember how I mentioned that certain Haïtians thought it was unseemly for a Catholic school student to be out fishing? Well, I'd like those people to know that not once but two times has Cardinal Roger M. Mahoney come to eat at my restaurant. His Eminence is the Archbishop in charge of the Archdiocese of Los Angeles. Another customer took a photograph of the cardinal and me. Let me tell you: that picture is framed and hung up with great pride. Cardinal Mahoney ate chicken both visits. He loved it.

APPETIZERS

TIMALIS SAUCE

NOT SO LONG AFTER my restaurant opened for business, a guy was calling out my name, "TiGeorges."

For someone to call me TiGeorges makes sense because it's my nickname, and it's part of the name of the restaurant. But this guy pronounced it perfectly, and had a good accent. I said to myself, "This person definitely must know me." Then I turned around and it was a white guy who I'd never met before. I said, "Wow, how do you know my name so well?" He said, "I've been to your country several times. My friend was the ambassador there and we used to hang out. I love your country."

This guy and I spoke for a while and when it was time to order, he said, "There's this one thing I had in Haïti, a sauce called *timalis* sauce. I'm gonna eat whatever you serve me, but I really want you to fix some timalis sauce."

Okay. It would be a real insult to tell this gentleman, "No, I don't have the stuff." To tell you the truth, it would be a real embarrassment for me, a Haïtian, to be more ignorant about my own cuisine—here at the only Haïtian restaurant around—than this fair-skinned American man.

I went to the back of the restaurant, walked out by the back door—I pretended to take out the trash or something—and I started pacing around. I thought and I thought. "Timalis sauce?" I asked myself. "What is timalis?" Over and over I asked myself. Then, I remembered. We have a children's story in Haïti. About Malis and Bouki. Bouki is the stupid guy. And Timalis is the "little malice," the vicious guy, always doing bad things to Bouki.

So I'm trying to put this information together. There's a guy in my restaurant asking me to make timalis sauce, which I've never heard of. But in the children's story, if you're referring to Timalis, you're referring to someone malicious, someone hotheaded. So I went into the kitchen and I prepared a sauce. I put habanero chili in and the usual lime juice, onions, thyme, olive oil, and salt. I thought, "This is a white guy. And that habanero chili, that shit is extremely hot. I'm not gonna make it too hot for this guy." I served his meal and I put on this improvised guess at timalis sauce. Well, the guy says to me, "Georges, this is good, but it's not hot enough."

I said, "Holy shit!" What a guy! I went back to the kitchen, saying to myself, *Oh, this is the way he wants it? Well, I'm gonna let him have it!* I went in there and fixed something that even I wouldn't wanna eat. I brought the stuff out to the guy. Man, he was sweating! His nose was running. He was crying. "Georges," he said, "bring me more napkins." The guy ate and ate and ate. He finished the sauce. He cleaned his plate. He pushed back from the table, this grand gesture. Then he said, "TiGeorges, that's what you call a timalis sauce! The stuff is good! Put it on the menu."

So I did. That was one hell of an endorsement.

I can't stop laughing, thinking back to that guy. I've had so many remarkable customers over the years, and from all kinds of backgrounds. And of course, that's the beautiful thing about Los Angeles—so many cultures come together, so many geographies. Of course, yes, sure, sometimes those tectonic plates cause earthquakes. Some days are for hot sauce. Other times, sweet plantains.

I first arrived in LA on August 16, 1981. I traveled cross-country in my brand new pride and joy, a Renault LeCar. I'd just graduated from the School of Visual Arts. I'd started out at Kingsborough Community College in Brooklyn. I did a semester at NYU. It took me seven years to get through school because I had to help my mother and my siblings. I owned the cab. Whenever I could take the time and had the money, I'd go back for the next semester. We all did what we had to. My sister, Danielle, she had a part-time job at a fast food burger place. She earned twenty dollars per week. I used to tell my sister, "Danielle, you gotta do better! That twenty dollars ain't gonna cut it!" She went out and landed a job at the leading payroll processing firm. Big salary. And when the company decided to move to New Jersey and she didn't want to go, she received a twenty-two-thousand-dollar severance. She took the money and opened Sassie Hair Salon. She still owns and operates the shop, out on Long Island.

In 1981, when I left for the West Coast, I departed from Long Island. Then I stopped in Baltimore, Maryland, to see my brother Eddie. And then, I went to Norfolk, Virginia, where my brother Wilson was working, building submarines. After I left those guys behind, I was all alone. Then life, reality, set in. I was no longer home. I was already a twenty-seven-year-old guy, and living at home at that age was abnormal for an American. I woke up one morning and knew it was time to move on with my life, to start building something for myself.

I was driving alone in Kansas when I got a speeding ticket. I was so many miles away from my destination. I was lonely. I was depressed. I spotted a guy who looked to be about my age, holding a cardboard sign. The sign read, "CA." I drove by, then realized that was the abbreviation for California. I pulled onto the shoulder, backed up, and asked this hitchhiker if he was heading west. "Yes I am," he said. "Well," I said, "hop in."

He and I spent fifteen hundred miles together. But you know what's funny? I never asked him his name! When he got in the car, the first thing he told me was, "As of now, you don't spend your money. I'm buying everything."

So, as we went along, this guy would direct me to stop at different places. On occasion, he took me to places where black guys weren't welcome. He was white. A real interesting guy. He'd say, "Georges, I'm going to take you to a place where, since you're black, people are not going to want to see you. I don't want you to look at them, don't make eye contact. We gonna go eat. And then we gonna leave. I guarantee you, it's gonna be okay." And indeed, at this one place, there were a whole bunch of lily whites, people in their seventies, very old and conservative people. They made me feel I was not welcome. But as a Haïtian man, I don't usually worry about racism. My attitude is, if he's a racist, that's his problem. Not mine.

That said, I was nervous enough already. I'd decided not to drive too far south because in New York some of my friends had said, "If you're black and you go to the Deep South, you may run into trouble." But they were talking about Interstate 40. They were talking about Alabama. Nobody was talking about the prairie and Mountain West states.

That restaurant was on the I-70. I think in Kansas. Somewhere before Colorado. I remember Colorado well because my hitchhiker ran out of money. The Renault was climbing into Denver—you know about the mile-high altitude. My hitchhiker wanted to make money by selling some blood. He said, "Georges, we need some money to breathe." I said, "Well, I still have some money, and I'm not gonna sell blood." So now, whatever money I had left, it looked like I was gonna have to spend.

While we were going through Colorado, closing in to Arizona, we bumped into two blonde girls. "We're going to the Grand Canyon," one of the girls said. "Do you guys want to come?" We said yes, and we followed them. In the process, a big rig almost flattened us. The girls had quickly switched roads, but I wasn't watching closely and I slowed down quickly so I wouldn't miss the exit. The big rig was coming fast behind me, air brakes roaring. I was lucky to swerve out of the way.

We made it to the Grand Canyon. I was still shaken, really nervous, about the near-accident. The hitchhiker says to me, "We're going with the girls, down to the bottom of the Canyon." I thought, "This is a man I picked up because he was holding a cardboard sign. I don't even know his name! What if he wakes up in the middle of the night and runs away with my Renault?" I said to him, "You can go with these girls. I'm going to sleep in the car."

So he went down, and I stayed up. About five or six in the morning, he knocked on the window. He said, "Hey, Georges, guess what? You thought I was going to steal your car? You got scared!" I said, "Yeah, I got spooked." And he said, "Man, it was great." He probably had an affair with those two girls.

We hit the road again, the hitchhiker and I. When we arrived at Las Vegas, we made a pit stop. I remember my brother Wilson saying, "Georges, if your air conditioning doesn't work, you're gonna have problems crossing that deep Nevada desert." Wilson was right—it was hot, a dry heat unlike anything I was used to back in Haïti, or for that matter, New York. The AC kept pumping, though. Whoever said the French can't build a decent car?

We weren't long for Vegas. We were so close now to California that I had no interest in going to play casino games or see some showgirls. We had a burger and a soda from some stand on the city's outskirts. Then, Golden State, here we come.

☼ ☼ ☼

I DROPPED THE HITCHHIKER off near Pomona. All in all, he was good company. So here I was—in California! I had managed to keep three hundred dollars of my road money—so that was my stake, my seed money for a whole new life. Hmm.

I stayed with my uncle Abner. A real wise guy. Abner was well-connected in the construction industry.

He'd been in it for thirty-five years and knew all the big boys. His health wasn't great—he'd had that wall fall on him when he was younger. He ended up passing at age sixty-five. But he lived thirty or forty years with only one lung, because the other had been removed due to severe pulmonary problems. I don't know for certain if this condition was related to what happened in the bakery, in Haïti.

Uncle Abner lived in Santa Monica, a few miles from the ocean. I didn't see any toy boats carved out of coconuts, but I did see kids flying kites. Abner offered to get me a job in construction. I declined because my mind was set on film. I felt that I had to pursue the chance to make films in Hollywood. That's what my schooling was for. That's why I came out west. Well, I didn't succeed. And for a while, I'd ask myself every day, "Should I take a job with Uncle Abner?"

Part of my heart will always remain in New York—that was my introduction to America. But I love Los Angeles—especially the weather. What can I say, Haïtians and colder climates—not a great mix. The weather is one thing, the entertainment industry, another. Truly, sadly, I wasn't cut out for the Hollywood life. When I arrived out here, weekday mornings I would go stand outside the studios, or hang out in restaurants and fast food joints nearby the studios, always hoping to bump into people who worked in the film business. I figured, then I'd just need to fill out an application, and I'd be a cameraman in no time. Of course, that isn't how things work. One has to suffer to make it in Hollywood. And one must have a parent with the money to support you until you don't need help anymore. If you're a starving artist, by the time you make it, you'll be destroyed. I didn't have money in my pocket. I had a car note to pay. I just couldn't see myself going down that avenue.

That realization didn't at all diminish my lifelong love of the cinema. In Port-de-Paix, the city hall sometimes doubled as a movie theater. There was this Frenchman named Alain who organized the screenings. I was a kid, and Alain loved me very much. Everyone else had to pay to get in to see the best films—the John Waynes, the Clint Eastwoods—Alain let me attend for free.

Well, not really free. Because Alain would want me to help him splice. The film would arrive on multiple reels and we would have to string them together. That's where I learned about editing, with Alain telling me, "You cannot cut it this way because you're going to have a jump." Or, "Do it this way or you'll have missing sound." Or, "You'll destroy the lip-synching, the synchronization." All that I learned by the age of eight or nine years old, thanks to the Frenchman.

Movies and food. Two of my lifelong loves. When I first moved to Brooklyn in 1970, I remember on Eastern Parkway—at Franklin and Eastern Parkway, right by the train station—there was an American diner. I used to love going there. I was particularly into eggs. I always wanted eggs over easy, which seemed so exotic to me.

I used to sit at the counter, watching the short order cook prepare me eggs and hash browns. I'd add a glass of orange juice on days when I could afford the extra fifteen cents.

Well, guess what? Soon after that, in 1972, my mother opened a restaurant in Brooklyn, one of the very first Haïtian-owned restaurants, on Church Avenue and Thirty-Third Street. I wanted to do the same thing I'd witnessed at that other diner—to cook eggs for customers, sunny side up or over easy. And quickly, I got my chance. What happened next might sound very racial, but it was not a racial thing!

There was this black guy who used to come in, who wanted sunny-side-up. And then another guy, a white guy, walked in, and he wanted scrambled. The black guy's order arrived first. But I executed the scrambled first because, for me, it was a lot easier. Because even as I'd observed and dreamed of making eggs sunny-side-up, I was terrible at doing it. It required ingenuity and dexterity to flip those two eggs! Those eggs would have to be cooked at a certain temperature prior to them being turned. I was nervous. My brother Michael was the expert at this, but he wasn't around. I made the scrambled eggs first, buying time to see if Michael might return. He didn't. So I served the white guy first. And the black guy was pissed. Here I am, fresh off the plane from Haïti, not fully understanding the black and white issues in America, and then you know, it's like I was lost, I was really lost. I wish I could find that guy today to apologize, to let him know that race wasn't a factor. I was just afraid to ruin his eggs. Now, the good news was that black guy ended up coming around almost daily, and sitting around and talking to us. But I never said "sorry."

My mom's diner failed. By 1974, we were out of business. We failed because we weren't prepared. We didn't grasp how much hard work it would take. We all counted on my brother Eddie to get stuff done, but brother Eddie had his own life. He wanted to move on, to become a great chef elsewhere. So Eddie left, my mom had two jobs, I was going to college part time, Michael was in high school, Taylor was running the register. Different brothers were working different hours. Eddie, when he was still there, would open. Michael would come. Then my mother, after she finished the hospital shift. Oh, the poor lady, she must have been so tired. Then I'd come. Then Taylor.

The restaurant struggled for another reason. We weren't Americans, but we were selling American food. We offered some Haïtian dishes, but mostly, classic American diner food—which, let's face it, we didn't really know how to properly prepare. We said we were an "American Haïtian" place, but looking back, if we'd said we were only Haïtian, and we'd focused on cuisine we knew so well, and could make so well, then that restaurant would have survived and thrived. As it happened, our clientele were mainly Anglos. They didn't care much about Haïti, and they expected

American food. And here I am, a Haïtian guy who can't even flip two eggs.

When my mom bought the restaurant, the place basically came with one employee. His name was Maurice. He was a white guy, and he did his best to coach us how to do the pot roast, the meat loaf, all the American foods. So here we are, Haïtians, having some problems learning to speak the language, located in a neighborhood where not to say we weren't welcome, but we were something so different that people had question marks. And maybe some of them had a little bit of fear. Although a Jewish guy who lived in the apartment below us fell in love with and married my older sister Marie-Carle, who was back staying with us after just graduating from McGill University. We welcomed him into the family, that's for certain! But all in all, our language problems and our being different probably wasn't the ideal recipe for an enterprise's long-term success.

I've learned from those Brooklyn mistakes. First of all, I can flip one hell of an egg! But more importantly, here in Echo Park, at TiGeorges' Chicken, I do not hide from being Haïtian. I trumpet it! I fly the flag—literally—out front. I think establishing this identity has really truly helped me. I've received much media attention, and the general public knows if they're looking for Haïtian cuisine, or Haïtian culture, where to come. It's a niche, compared to running a diner. But it's an important niche. And, hey, culinary cross-culturalism takes time. The very first American meal I ate was during the airplane flight from Haïti to New York. In Haïti, of course, we put spices on everything, and color in everything. I mean, strong spices, bright colors. Here we were on the airplane, and the food we're served is bland and gray. I think we were served a mashed potato, a foodstuff unknown in Haïti. There was a tan gravy on top of the potato. Oh man, we didn't know what that was! And there was the chicken—all white meat. And a bit of iceberg lettuce salad. Oh no. I was not going to consume any of that. My sister Danielle was looking at me and I was looking back at her, and we knew damn well that we were not touching that food! But we were so happy coming here to see our mother and our brothers who were already in America, so eating was a distant thought. We were more worried about air pockets, since the plane was dropping every five or ten minutes. Let me tell you: I thought riding in the mountains on top of a Haïtian bus was bouncy. That's got nothing on turbulence at thirty thousand feet!

It took me two or three years to begin to understand what American food is really all about. Where do I go to eat steak? Where are the different kinds of barbeque places? Those in particular would remind me of Haïti—the open fires, the flavorful roasting of meats. Other meals were way more foreign. Like knishes—and hey, who doesn't like knishes? I fell in love with knishes. I used to go to Coney Island. I'd see the water and the carny attractions. And I'd go to Nathan's and have a potato knish with mustard. Sheesh. I'd eat three or four knishes during a night. Even today, we don't have knishes like that out on the West Coast. But whenever I get to New York, if I happen to be near the Coney Island area, I'll go enjoy that good knish.

Oh, sure I loved Coney Island. And Nathan's. Those French fries! Another thing that turned me on. Not the famous hot dogs, though. I was not too crazy about hot dogs. In high school, the way hot dogs were served, with sauerkraut—imagine, you just landed from Haïti and now they're giving you hot dogs with sauerkraut! Oh man, I didn't care for that stuff. I would give this one big guy named Charlot my dog with kraut in exchange for his lemon cake. That'd be my lunch, lemon cake. I'd still make that trade. Charlot?

I never worked at Nathan's, but I did work at two fast food places, one in LA—more on that later—and a place in New York called Winston's. It was on Empire Boulevard in Flatbush. It was my first job, I was making like twenty-two dollars per week. Because I had a car, and gas was twenty-three cents per gallon, I'd use my Winston's earnings and invite my friends to take weekend trips. There I was, I couldn't speak a word of English, and I'm flipping burgers in the back. Oh man, I was so good at it. Then Elias, the Greek guy who ran the place, he told me, "I'm going to put you on the cash register." I said, "Holy cow." I couldn't believe it. I couldn't speak the language, but Elias trusted me to run the register. A customer would place an order, "I want five French fries, three Cokes, a couple of hamburgers, this and that," and I'd tally everything and try to collect the bill. The customer would say, "*Oh no no no. This is the money for the fries. This other guy has the money for the hamburgers.*" People would steal from Winston's, and at the end of the night, my register would be short. That's something that doesn't happen in Echo Park. No splitting of checks, please.

I can't talk Brooklyn and food without talking about pizza. In Haïti, there was no such thing. Probably today you'll find some. But when I was growing up—pizza? What is this? When I came to America, like everyone else, I loved pizza. On Franklin Avenue, for thirty-five cents, I'd get a Kool-Aid and a slice. Man, that pizza was good. You know New York pizza: fold that slice over itself, keep a couple napkins in your hand, let that fat or grease drip all over your pants. So good!

Steak is another food I associate with America, and with New York in particular. One of my uncles introduced me to Tad's Steaks in Times Square. It was a big thing for me to go eat T-bone steak at Forty-Second Street. The cost was like $2.65. With six dollars, I would have the greatest Times Square afternoons. Coming from Haïti, being able to enjoy life at that level, that was truly an amazing experience. That was 1971, 1972. I'd go every Saturday. In 1973, I graduated from high school, and moved on to college. At that point I stopped going to Tad's.

Over the years, Dominican food has been big in New York's boroughs. But you know something, I don't every recall eating at a Dominican restaurant outside of the Dominican Republic. The first time I ever visited Haïti's neighbor, I had such a great experience. You go there, and you forget about reality. The food. The music. Everything is *live, live, live.* You know how they say, "Live from New York…"? Well, they can say, "Live from the Dominican Republic," because they take entertainment seriously.

During my trip, I was supposed to meet my cousin at a particular beach. I got lost and I ended up at a different beach in a place called Puerto Plata, in the north of the country. When I got there, I realized, "Oh, man, wrong place, no cousin." My mother was with me and so were some of my other cousins. We were sitting in my car, and the policeman guarding the beach walked over to us. He said, "C'mon guys, you don't have to go far. We have pleasure. We have everything here. We have entertainment."

I said to myself, "Where the hell is the guy going to find entertainment?" Man, the guy removed his uniform. He went into a hut, he brought out an accordion, and he told us, "Georges, whatever you want, we got it here. From whiskey to beer, you name it. From lobster to red snapper. Crab. We gonna fix dinner." And the guy didn't even ask us if I had money or not, but he assumed that, hey, I'm driving a car, coming from Haïti, and above all, coming from the United States, I'm gonna have money. Let me tell you: it was about four o'clock when we got there and about nine o'clock when I remembered again that we were supposed to be looking for my cousin! I told the guy I wanted to see the bill, and he gave it to me. It was fifty dollars. There was no way in the world you could have such great pleasure for that little amount of money. And then guess what? The party was not over. Eventually, I connected with my cousin—I drove to meet him. My cousin was in a car with a whole bunch of Germans, enjoying good times just like we were. Their car had broken down, their battery had failed. Once they received a jump, they found us and the party resumed.

In Los Angeles and elsewhere these days, Haïti and the Dominican are considered to be colocated on the island of Hispaniola. Well, ask a Haïtian what "Hispaniola" means, and he'll say, "Haïti." Remember, Haïti ruled the whole island for a quarter-century. In the eighteen hundreds, the Dominican was under Haïtian governance.

Of course, Haïti was at one time occupied by the French, until Toussiant L'Ouverture and everyone tossed them out. And previously, Haïti—the whole island—was called *La Pequeña España* or "Little Spain." Very few people know that. When people hear a Haïtian speak Spanish, they'll ask, "How does a Haïtian know Spanish?" Excuse me? If we're talking about Spanish, truly, Haïti came first. Before Cuba. Before Mexico.

Before Central America. Before South America. Before all of Latin America.

The Dominican has been a separate country from Haïti since 1844. Many Dominicans hate that Haïti is responsible for them being black—the Dominicans have never accepted the fact that they are a black society. That's my belief. And because there's a breakdown of cultural exchange, there is not much interaction between the people of the two nations. We've learned their music, their language, but only to a small degree. That's more, though, than they have learned of us. You will find Haïtians who speak Spanish, but how often do you meet a Dominican who speaks Kreyol? A friend of mine who is a sports fan pointed something else out. To him, Haïtians and Dominicans are coming from the same island, with the same weather and seasons. "So, why," this guy asked me, "do all the *beisbol* players come from the Dominican and none from Haïti?" Easy. Divided island. Spanish vs. French. Spanish-speaking countries play beisbol. French-speaking countries don't.

When my family left Haïti and moved to Brooklyn, that's when I started to meet and spend more time with Dominicans. Funny, huh? We traveled all that distance just to meet our neighbors. When we were living on 284 Eastern Parkway, there were lots of Dominican families. One of the guys, called Flaco, was a classmate of mine at Erasmus Hall High School. Flaco was a great swimmer—actually, his entire family were great swimmers. Flaco was my first Dominican acquaintance.

His mom used to call out to him, "Flaco! Flaco! Flaco!" from her apartment window.

I got along fine. Remember, one of my nicknames was "Zo," skinny as a bone. So Flaco and I were both thin young dudes.

In Haïti, I spoke Kreyol and French and I had to learn Latin for Catholic school and mass. English, it took me a couple of years to pick up, once we arrived in the States. Spanish, I think I was fluent within ten years. I married a Spanish-speaking woman, a native of El Salvador, in 1983. We visited Salvador the next year. A year after that, I was speaking without needing her translation help. The marriage didn't endure, but thanks to my ex, we opened up the party supplies rental business with an emphasis on attracting Spanish-speaking customers. This was an underserved market—I'd identified it as such at the party supplies business where I briefly worked prior to opening our own. Even my mediocre—back then—Spanish was a useful business skill. When we'd take a phone order, my ex would listen in and in case I didn't understand a word, she'd write its meaning in English for me on a piece of paper. By the time I got fluent, look out! Today, on any given shift at TiGeorges' Chicken, you'll hear catch me chattering away in all four tongues.

My marriage didn't last, but two really truly wonderful sons came from our union, my great boys Benjamin and Michael! When the family was all together, we loved going away weekends. We were always getting onboard a plane, or driving somewhere. My kids loved that so much. We used to go to Laughlin, Nevada. Ben and Mike were very small. When it came to finding lodging, I always played things by ear—no reservations. This one holiday weekend we went out there, and everything was booked. The Flamingo? Booked. The Best Western, even. Booked. The deskman there, he said to me, "Sir, I have a mobile home. Do you want to rent it?" I said, "Why not?" I looked at that mobile home, and it wasn't the greatest, but I was going to spend three nights in Laughlin, and I was not going to have toddlers sleep in the car. So I said, "Yes, we accept the trailer." He called it a mobile home. But to me, it was more like a trailer. We climbed into the trailer and Ben looked around. He must have been four or five years old. He knew we didn't normally stay in a place like this. Ben said, "Dad, you trying to tell me there's no room in the big hotel?" Ha! My sons already had a taste of the good things. Georges Laguerre was making it in America.

SQUASH SOUP

MY GRANDMOTHER WAS NAMED Suzanna Pierre-Vincent.

She died very old. I never, ever saw her sick. Once, she was bleeding internally and she went to see the doctor. But guess what? She used to take aspirin every morning. The doctor said, "Mrs. Suzanna, there's nothing wrong with you. Your heart is like an eighteen-year-old girl's. You simply have to stop taking these aspirins."

Grandma Suzanna Pierre lived into at least her late nineties. Haïtians of a certain age didn't always receive birth certificates, and some members of our family claimed that my grandmother lived to be 104 years old. She was in the neighborhood, anyway. She was at least ninety-eight.

Back then in Haïti, record-keeping was not up to par. Especially if you were born in the mountains. My grandmother was not born in a city. She was a peasant and her family didn't have any money. People wouldn't go to city hall to get their records made until they had saved enough gourdes. So a person could be six or eight years old and never have been officially recorded as being alive. My grandmother was likely in this category.

That's an assumption. These certificates that'd be issued years after the fact, they'd be based on hearsay. "Oh, I know you were born on this day or that day." The person could bring a witness. Or, the person could come alone and submit any information they wanted, and it was up to the clerk to accept or reject or modify the claim. And for a person who couldn't read or write, he or she would have to hope that the clerk was putting down what the person requested. There weren't many checks and balances, or efficiencies in the record-keeping system.

I owe so much to my grandmother. She was truly a person with a great heart. She never got mad. And her work ethic was incredible. I think she's made me what I am today. All of my siblings and my cousins, everyone depended on her. Those who she could help send to school, she helped. Those who she could find jobs for, she did. My grandmother never moved here to join the rest of us. She never wanted to. In Haïti, she had an occupation. She was independent. And she definitely didn't like the cold. She did come early on to spend time with Uncle Melcourt, her son. He lived in Akron, Ohio. That was the home of Firestone, the tire company. Grandma Suzanna Pierre used to look at the tires on vehicles in Haïti. Most were Michelin, a French tire. Others were Goodyear or Dunlop. When she'd spot a Firestone, she'd say, "I know where those tires were manufactured." The only English-language words she knew were, oddly enough, "fresh fish." Ohio has a lot of lakes. And I guess maybe back in the fifties, people would sell their daily catch in trucks by the side of the road? Or go door-to-door? That's the impression my grandma got, anyway. So she used to holler, "Fresh fish! Fresh fish!" just like she was on the sidewalks, slinging fritay.

I keep a photograph of my grandmother up on the restaurant wall closest to the kitchen. She was such a great chef. She was famous for her squash soup.

On Sundays in Haïti, everyone consumes squash soup. Mass would begin at 4:00 a.m., to keep everyone out of the heat. Squash soup would be served immediately afterwards, by 5:30 or 6:00 a.m. The mass, by the way, was made back then in Latin. My mother knew every word by heart. I learned but I no longer remember how to say *Spiritus Sanctus* and all the rest. Today, that mass is held in Kreyol or French.

People would dress up for mass. Once, in another interview with the *Los Angeles Times*, I made a remark about how Haïtians can be the poorest, can be living in the ghetto, but when it comes to Sunday mornings, you'll find that every individual is wearing his or her best outfit. The best suit—dark, always blue, black, or brown. The best tie. The best underwear. The best shoes. The best haircut.

Getting up early enough for mass was never an issue. Some people would go party Saturday night and then go directly to church. Because to party in Haïti is not like to party in LA, where the revelry ends at one or two in the morning. In Haïti, parties begin around ten or eleven at night. People would dress up to go out, then have their good stuff on and just make way for church.

So people were hungry Sunday mornings, for different reasons. I said earlier that acra was the national dish of Haïti. Well, we have another: squash soup. The squash soup that my grandmother prepared was a long process. You know how it was in Haïti. In those days, we didn't have supermarkets where you could go to one central location and find everything. Instead, we were always heading out looking for the freshest products, at the best prices, and they'd be available from different sources. There's a little town called Shansolme located about six kilometers from Port-de-Paix. Tuesdays, my grandmother would travel there to buy meat and bones—the soup required bone marrow. My grandmother would marinate the meat on

Wednesday, then boil it on Thursday. She'd boil it until all the nerves attached to the bone were loosened—disconnected, actually. What an incredible aroma! By Thursday evening, we'd already know around our house that she was going to have a great batch of soup ready for Sunday.

At my restaurant, I follow my grandmother's practice. I marinate four days prior to serving. I use the ingredients she used, starting with the squash, of course. My grandmother used to go to another town's weekly market, held on Friday, to buy her squash. Saturdays, she would peel the squash. Since squash has such a hard surface, this peeling takes a while, and she'd accept help from any of us in the family who offered. Later on Saturday, she'd boil the squash and a few other vegetables she'd add—carrots, celery, green onions. She'd do this at about 5:00 p.m., after my mother had closed up her bakery and the general store. Once the kitchen became available, it was my grandmother's turn to commandeer that stove. Sunday morning, just prior to the crowds coming after church, she'd add the habanero and Scotch bonnet chilies and the lime.

She'd be tasting all Sunday morning. She'd say, "This chili is not good enough. This Scotch bonnet is not good enough." The aroma from that Scotch bonnet really enhanced the flavor. Sunday mornings, she'd have three people helping her and the end result of these six days of work—from the Tuesday market trip onwards—would be a forty-gallon vat of this incredible squash soup.

Customers would arrive, and two hours later she'd be sold out. And guess what? People would still be standing in line, holding their pots and their other containers, looking forlorn. "Hey," we'd say, "come earlier next week."

Many people would sit down in our kitchen, or on the couple of tables we'd set up outside, and eat their soup on our property. The rest, who brought those takeaway pots and the like, you know, I never knew how my grandmother decided what to charge them. She'd look at the size of their containers and say, "That's a five-gourde bowl." Or, "That's a two-gourde bowl." I think she was very haphazard. I'm sure she shortchanged herself by not having standard pricing and standard measurements. This is something that even today in Haïti is still in existence. I think the government and the people take it for granted. I think that this is something they all ought to pay more attention to. You simply cannot continue indefinitely as a society where you are forever purchasing things via unmeasured containers.

Change would be good for Haïti's businesses. And for international trade. It also would have helped my siblings and me, way back when. My grandmother wouldn't allow any of us to eat even one spoonful of squash soup until after she'd made back what she spent. If she'd spent five hundred gourdes, we had to wait to eat until she made five hundred gourdes. This policy probably affected my brother Harry the most. Harry could never wait for anything, he was always in a hurry.

So by 6:00 a.m., he just had to go fishing. That's when the delaqet bite, right? So on occasion, Harry would sneak out the back while my grandmother was at the crucial moment with the soup. This would piss her off! She might have needed his help. The rest of us, we stuck around both to help and also out of self-interest—as soon as she hit the break-even point, it was soup time for us. Harry—by the time he came back, the soup would be long gone.

My grandmother was held in high standing as the best squash soup maker in the state, hey, maybe the whole country. Everyone came by to consume that stuff. The health inspector, the chief of police, all the dignitaries. The health inspector was always welcome. Suzanna Pierre did her cooking right out in the open, where you could see everything that was happening. It was not like in an American home, where the kitchen isn't usually the focal point.

I'm leaving something important out of the story. Something my family doesn't talk much about. Something I didn't learn about until late in life. Something I don't even know if it's true.

That is: my grandmother was likely having an affair with the mayor of our city.

My brother Taylor told me this. The way he said it was kind of cryptic. He said, "Do you know that city hall was built by our grandfather?" What did that mean? Like as a laborer? What he meant was, our grandfather was the mayor! As kids, we'd hear rumors like this. "So and so is your cousin. So and so is related to you." But that was the end of it, we never questioned it, we left it as is. It's not easy for me to bring this up. How did the affair happen, if it happened? My grandmother used to cook and sell out of our place. But her food was so great she was one day asked by a European guy, "Well, Mrs. Suzanna, would you like to come work for us?"

So she did. She went to work at the home of this wealthy guy, the most valuable businessman in town. She cooked for him and his guests. He was friendly with the mayor. The mayor would be out, socializing, eating supper at the businessman's house. Remarking about how brilliant the food tastes. My grandmother would have been well respected, having that job, plus being such a talented chef. One thing would have led to another, I guess.

Oh, our house was located in front of city hall. And ours was the best-built house in town. It was a stone and concrete building, lots of rebar, with a view of the old fort. How could our family have received access to these materials? How come this house was built in such proximity to the mayor's quarters? This is all I'll say about this topic, because again, it's speculative. I don't know the full story. Hopefully, someone who knows more will read this and contact me, and either correct me or add in more details. Was my mother's father the mayor?

Speaking of prominent politicians and Port-de-Paix, I should mention at least briefly another of my childhood neighbors. I knew of this guy mostly because he had a very old American car. He kept it parked in his driveway. He never drove it anywhere. But every morning, he would turn the ignition and start the vehicle. Then he'd turn the car off.

Guess what? You'd never guess. This neighbor wound up becoming the President of Haïti.

His name was Joseph Emile Jonassaint. He was born the same year as my father. He also lived next door to city hall in a very nice house most likely built by the French. It had gardens and lots of trees in the yard.

Jonassaint was a lawyer, a judge, and a very conservative guy. Seldom would he walk the streets, only if he was headed to the courthouse or to the college where he used to teach. He was a tall man, and we'd see him on weekends standing behind his gate, peering outside to see what was happening in the neighborhood.

This man was president for five months during 1994. He was the fiftieth president and the only one from our city. He was a temporary leader during a sadly, typically troubled time for Haïti. Anything else about him, we ain't gonna talk about.

PÂTÈ DE POULET

N 1979, I RETURNED to Haïti to shoot my SVA thesis film. It was titled *Haïti em Couleur—Haïti in Color*. It was about Carnival.

That was the second film I'd done. The first was about a man who dreams his own death. He goes to sleep and dreams that he's dying. Then he wakes up and has a heart attack. It was named the semester's best film.

For the thesis project, I told my film school buddies I was going to Haïti to shoot. Five of those buddies agreed to come with me.

Filming turned out to be a difficult proposition. Our equipment was late arriving because it was Carnival season and the planes were overcrowded. So, I didn't have the time and gear to do everything I'd planned— and we had a low budget, as well. I did my very best, though. I shot the Carnival. Carnival is truly something that Haïtians take very seriously. It's like what Brazil has or Mardi Gras in New Orleans—every February. A guy will lift weights all year long, waiting for Carnival season, just to display his muscles, to show how strong that he is, how big of a torso he has.

The finished film is just sitting in the can. Hopefully one day it will end up being a small piece of historical information valuable to the next generations in Haïti, showing what Carnival was like back then.

My college buddies, they still remember. During the decades since, they've told me some version of the following: that trip left Haïti implanted in their hearts, souls, minds, and of course, in their bellies. Take, for instance, my dear friend Arlene. She was my girlfriend at the time of our trip, and she was the film's assistant director. All these years later, Arlene came to visit my restaurant. She told me how in 1979, one food in particular had made such an impression on her.

"TiGeorges, man," Arlene told me, "don't forget to put *pâtè de poulet* on your menu."

I said, "Well, people are not going to like that dish."

"Georges! I still love that stuff," she said. "You gotta add it."

And guess what? Arlene was correct. It's a knockout dish. It's not something that I make all the time, but it's something I truly enjoy doing. And when certain people come to my restaurant, if I don't have the pâtè de poulet, hey, that's it. Big complaints from everybody in the know.

Pâtè. It's such a big thing in Haïti. We have beef pâtè. We have chicken pâtè. We have *morru pâtè*, which is catfish. Just to name a few. What's so great about pâtè? It's the dough. Some people simply cannot make the dough light—the dough has to be lighter than a croissant. It needs to be like sheets of paper, layers and layers and layers of thin filo dough. And when it's been baked, it should crumble.

Let me tell you: making pâtè is an art. The preparation of the dough takes hours. That's what we call in French *mille fueille*. And to do that it requires a lot of butter, a lot of lard. It is a fattening dish, but when you encounter somebody in Haïti who can do this—*ah-hah*! This is something that we Haïtians take great pride in. Am I good at it? Well, I can do it. And in my case, of course, I have learned from my brother Eddie. When were kids, man, that guy was good with pastry—and most other foods, too. Whenever there was a party in the neighborhood, if you needed someone to cook for you, you'd ask my brother Eddie.

In Haïti, we'd usually consume pâtè de poulet with black coffee. It's breakfast for us—we eat very light breakfasts in Haïti. In my era, we usually had jelly, bread and butter, or sometimes a small piece of cake. If not cake, then pâtè. You would see a guy going around selling pâtè. The guy would yell, "Pâtè! Pâtè! Hot pâtè!" Usually if you were sleeping late and you heard this guy, then you would make the effort to wake up. And guess what? If he was selling pâtè, by eight o'clock, that pâtè was either sold out or it was no good. It would have gone cold, it would no longer have the right flavor. Same as with my grandmother's soup. He'd sell out his product quickly. If he started selling at six o'clock in the morning, by eight o'clock he was nowhere to be found. So when you see me here in my restaurant, and you learn that, on occasion, my food runs out and I close early, understand that this is a concept that exists, truly, in the Haïtian culture. You finish selling, then you depart. Whatever you prepare, that's how much you're going to sell.

Back to the pâtè guy. People buying his item would bring their own bags for him to place it in. It's not like here in America, where you go buy something and it's served to you wrapped, and they give it to you in a plastic bag. Today, people complain about over-packaging. How materials are polluting the Earth. In Haïti, we recycled. We would have our own brown bag, or we'd have made a cloth bag. When we went shopping, we'd pull the bag out and use it. Pâtè was usually served on a little piece of paper. In Haïti—oh man, napkins? Those were not in existence. So basically the same paper that the pâtè man covered the food with in order to prevent flies or insects or any other animals from flirting with it, that would be the same paper he would then cut in small square pieces to serve the pâtè.

I'm sure everyone from Port-de-Paix remembers the pâtè guy, the way everyone remembers my grandmother for her squash soup. That guy would sing out, "Pâtè!" in such an impressive way. Definitely he had to be saying that with pride, because he knew he had such a great product. He would call out, "*Pat-tay; Pat-taaay; eh, Pat-taaay*" in different tones. He never forced you to buy. He never said, "I've got pâtè, would you like to buy some pâtè from me?" No. He would holler that he had pâtè. He knew few people could resist. He sold two pâtès, the twenty-five-cent pâtès and the fifty-cent pâtès, which was like half of a gourde.

The pâtè man—I cannot remember his name, but I remember his product, and his voice and his style. He carried a basket made of straw in his right arm, and he wore a straw hat. He was in his twenties. And again, let me tell you: on Sundays in particular, truly, he was the only guy to know to enjoy some good pâtè. He would have beef pâtè, and he would have bacalao, which is salted fish. Me, for some reason, I was always on the side of the beef.

Thinking about pâtè really makes me think again about my brother Eddie, who like I said, was so good with this and so many other foods. Let me tell you: I was always next to Eddie. Usually in the kitchen, but other times, too. Whatever he was into, I thought it must be the cool thing to do. For example, Eddie had a camera, but he very seldom took pictures. I would take the camera, go to the mountains with my buddies, and we'd take photos and then quietly return the camera. In my mind, Eddie was not going to realize who took the pictures. Was that stupid? Obviously. Of course he'd discover what we'd done after the picture had been printed. But Eddie never questioned the situation. Half of the time, though, I was the guy who took film to be developed—mostly so Eddie wouldn't so easily figure out what I was up to. And that's basically how I ended up learning photography. That love of photography started back then, when I was ten or eleven years old, and being both in awe of my brother and being sneaky, as well.

Photography wasn't his bag, but Eddie was always into cuisine. And I was his assistant. Eddie wound up working for some of the top hotels and for a top golf course. Oh man, I used to love going to work with my brother Eddie. Because my brother was the chef, and there I was in the kitchen next to him. I benefitted from that respect. The others would say, "Hey, Eddie's brother is in the room." Although I was the dishwasher, guess what? Once I finished washing dishes I would have the responsibility to do big tasks, and then people would come by and look at me like, "Oh, wait a minute? Hey, he's the chef's brother. He's also good. And he's also cleaning the pool and mowing the grass." And let me tell you: if you've never cut grass on a golf course, then you've never truly cut grass. You gotta wake up at like four o'clock in the morning, because during summertime, that grass really grows, man. You're constantly in the field, every day, mowing. There were spots where the big lawnmower couldn't get to, under trees and branches. So my job was to go around with a small hand-operated mower. I don't care how healthy you are, how strong of a man you are, carrying that machine around all day long in the heat and the humidity, well, after you do five or six trees, let me tell you: you'll have no energy left.

Soon, my brother Eddie put me in charge of the food stand at the pool. There was no money exchanged—it was a wealthy environment. Everybody brought coupons; that's how it was done. My job was to do the hamburgers. And then again, as the brother of the chef, I was in charge of doing all the tasks my brother delegated. On occasion there were big parties of five hundred people. Eddie would tell me to go check the plates, to make sure everything was clean. And you want to know something? Truly, truly—and I'm not saying this because he's my brother—people had great respect for Eddie's culinary abilities. But Eddie also had a crappy attitude. Crappy, crappy, let me tell you. A good brother, nice brother. A hard-working man. An honest man. But let me tell you: attitude, personality, *ahh*, Eddie, I know wherever you are you may not like what I'm about to say. I'm not going to give you a free ride. Although I love you, I love you. But brother, you were rough on people. When Eddie wanted something, man, people never wanted to give it to him. Why?

I don't know. Maybe he didn't know how to express himself, or maybe he couldn't tell people exactly what he really truly wanted. But he would send me out there as his brother because he would take so much pride in me, and because I had no trouble expressing myself. And I'm the man going in there making big decisions. "Hey, let me look at what's in there." Oh, okay. And I would go back and report to my brother Eddie. I would say quietly to him, "Hey Eddie, guess what? Everything is clean."

After those big parties, Eddie would take out a bottle of Scotch and we'd celebrate the job well done. The party guests would be so happy, enjoying every last bite of the meal. I feel the same way about my restaurant. I want you to clean your plate. Like Eddie used to say, "People don't eat your food, there's a reason."

Back at the golf course, on occasion, the owners would show movies. And guess what? The projector would break down—you know, the eight-millimeter projectors from back in the seventies? Since I was a film student, a filmmaker, I knew how to run all that stuff. On the golf course, when the machines would start acting up, I'd say, "I can fix it." The head man would say, "Are you sure, Georges?" I'd answer, "I am a filmmaker. Yes, I can fix it." And then I would. "Hey, *bravo*, Georges," the guy would say. So summers were about food and film and solving problems. And being with Eddie. And you want to know something? Way too soon, summer vacation would be over, and I'd be sad. Before driving or taking the Amtrak back to New York City, the people I'd worked with would say, "Oh, Georges, are you coming back with us next year? Please!" Well, I didn't wait until the next summer to return. Sometimes, things were so bad financially for us in New York that we couldn't afford enough food. I'd call Eddie and he'd say, "Hey, Georges, come down to Baltimore." Whatever food his job had that was going to expire, he'd give to us. My brother Michael and I would scrape together enough money to buy gas. We'd drive down on a Friday night or early Saturday morning. We'd spend a day or two with him, and load up the vehicle. If it was winter, we'd just put everything in the trunk—no reason to bring a cooler. A couple of trips, we brought home enough food to last a month. This is how the family survived. We Haïtians are willing to do things that other people won't. We going to hang in there, we going to tough it out, we going to stick together. Two dollars? Four or five brothers? We all going to eat.

A Haïtian immigrant I know recently told me a story. It was along these lines: "Hey, in New York City, there's this hospital janitor who is Haïtian. And guess what? His son is a doctor at the same hospital, doing heart operations, doing liver operations."

I remember when my dad came to America. My dad didn't speak any English. In Haïti, he'd been customs director and he'd had a coffee plantation and he'd had maids. Now he's in America, with none of that. And here, when my dad spoke English, man, you better run. Let me tell you: it was so embarrassing to hear my dad. In his mind, he would think, "Oh, I speak English." *Ahh,* his grammar was horrible. Yet, he took such a great pride in speaking the language. He didn't care how bad he was. The same was true for my mother. She had a car—she bought a station wagon at an auction. My brother Wilson was the first in the family to get a license, and then he and my brother Harry taught me to drive. They showed me all the rules of the game. Always keep your distance from trucks. Do not tailgate a bigger vehicle. Recognize who has the priority. So my mother bought the wagon, and it became my job to take her to work. Not the diner she bought, this is the graveyard shift at the hospital, I'm talking about the nursing gig. I mean, it was horrible. After school she was always preparing food. Saturdays, we were always getting up early in the morning to pick her up from her shift. The drill was to pick her up at eight o'clock in the morning, and from there we'd go do the week's shopping.

One winter morning, with Michael in the passenger's seat, I headed out to pick up mom. It had sleeted the night before and the road was really slippery, really icy. I had very little experience driving in these conditions—I'm from the tropics, man! So I hit a frozen patch of road, and the car swerved. I stepped on the brake, and of course, that made things worse and we started spinning. Eventually I hit a parked car, a 1972 Cadillac Fleetwood. It was brand new. Painted white, with white walls, white tires, and mahogany interior.

Oh, I hit that hot car so badly. And guess what? This Caddy was owned by a pimp.

Now, here I am, a nice guy. I said, "Well, Michael, why don't you go call the police, you know, we have to make a report."

Let me tell you: Michael said, "Georges, you got to be insane! You gonna call the police? Man, you better get out, because if that pimp come to find out that we fucked up his car, we are going to be buried alive!"

You know what? That made sense to me. We got out of there! We went to pick up my mother from work that day, told her we'd had an accident—without mentioning the detail about the pimp—and then we went shopping, dropped mom off, and then I took the car directly to the body shop.

Yes, that car we crashed into was a new Fleetwood. It was owned by the pimp who used to live next door to us on Eastern Parkway. He was a tall, black American man. Very handsome. Always wearing a hat. He always had the finest looking girls in the neighborhood. You know, you come from Haïti and you see this—let me tell you: this was really new to a Haïtian seventeen-year-old guy. We didn't speak much English, and the pimp didn't ever talk to us. But on occasion, he'd walk by and nod to us. That was our relationship with the man. But we knew he was a pimp—we used to see what the pimp used to do with the girls on President Street, which was a quiet street, with very little activity. I would see the pimp really giving those girls orders.

When I hit that pimp's car, it was like six o'clock in the morning. It was dark. I was tired. I was a little shook up. And, really, I was afraid. Some of that fear was because when my siblings and I were in high school, we used to be called "Frenchie" by many of our black American classmates. When they saw a Haïtian guy, they'd say: "Hey, yo, Frenchie!" Oh man, let me tell you: even today, you call me "Frenchie" you bring back bad memories. I am not French! But because we spoke French, because we came from a country that spoke French, in some people's closed minds, then we were French. Let me make this clear. We are familiar with the French culture because the French occupied us. But we are not French. We are Haïtian. So that morning of the accident, in addition to the genuine damage we'd just done, I guess I thought racism was gonna be a problem, too. I thought that if that guy knew it was a Haïtian guy who had sabotaged his car to that level—basically the car was totaled—then the guy was going to break my rib, break my leg, break my jaw, just dismantle me to the point where I would probably, definitely, become handicapped!

So my brother Michael, he was wiser. He had book smarts and street smarts. Michael knew right there and then that I was in the hand of hell that morning. So Michael told me, "Georges, we have to push away." Look at me, an innocent guy. It's an accident, I've got insurance. Why don't I call the police? Michael said, "No! This guy doesn't deal with the police. You gonna call the police? *Noooo*. You better get the hell out of here. Because one, the police would file a legal report, but because the guy knows it was you who hit, who destroyed his car, he is gonna come back some other time, some other day, to really truly do you harm."

I thank Michael very much, and I'm truly sad Michael is no longer with us today. He passed away from cancer—he had leukemia. He was forty-two years old, the same age my brother Eddie was when he passed away.

Let me get back to happier topics, to the pimp car story. So yes, we were insured. But after the accident, I was waiting and waiting to receive the insurance money to then hand over to the body shop on 116th Street. But the agent is giving me the runaround. I told my mom, "They will not give me the money." She said, "Okay, baby, we gonna go and collect that money."

My mother came with me the next time to the insurance office. The receptionist said, "You'll have to come back tomorrow, the adjuster is not here." Okay. We went back. "Well, I'm sorry Mrs. Laguerre, it's not happening today, you're going to have to come back." This happened yet again. This time, my mother decided, that's enough. Her English was only slightly better than my father's. My mother would speak loudly in English. She didn't care much about grammar—whether she mixed past, future, or present participles. Really, my mom went back into that insurance office speaking the most broken English in the world. Oh, but the way she spoke, the way she carried herself, she intimidated that adjustor. He said, "Mrs. Laguerre, could you wait for a second?" He walked off, then came back and handed my mother a check.

I look back and realize, never mind that she couldn't speak much English. It wasn't about that. It was the nerve and the audacity she exhibited, that's what earned her the respect that probably a native-born speaker would have more immediately received. These are big things. Your parents come to America, can't speak a word of English, and yet they have pride. Again, that's us Haïtians. We don't speak the language? Trust me, we're going to find a way to get what we deserve. Ten kids to support? Become a nurse at Florence Nightingale. Work the graveyard shift. Make twelve thousand dollars and manage to keep all of us happy and healthy. That's the drill! That's the Haïtian way. We do what we gotta do.

For example, I was a New York taxi driver! This is a job that many Haïtians do in the United States. You find a lot of guys—some of them are doctors, engineers—and when they come here, they simply can't get those kinds of professional jobs. I drove for the Fifty-Seventh Street Taxicab Company. It was funny. It was like being a part of those same stories you used to see on that old TV show *Taxi*. The dispatcher would always scream at you, yelling stuff like, "Hey, where are you? You're due in at 6:00 a.m.!" I would try to get morning hours, and they'd say, "No! Morning hours are for the veterans, guys that have been with the company for so long." So they would give me the crappy shifts, like weekends or late nights. But I was going to college. I had the energy. After a while, I ended up owning my own taxi. They called them liveries, or gypsy cabs. Mine was a 1970 Plymouth Fury 3, a gas guzzler with bad brakes. Once, at the intersection of Flatbush and Atlantic avenues, I almost killed a group of pedestrians. My brakes failed and I laid on the horn and, thankfully, the people scattered. Yeah, this wasn't a yellow cab, and I didn't have one of the incredibly valuable New York City taxi medallions. As a livery from Brooklyn, I was forbidden to pick up a fare in Manhattan. Queens and the Bronx were okay. I went to college for seven years. I drove probably during five of those years. I stopped the day I got robbed by a seventeen-year-old kid. He pulled out a gun and he told me to move over. I thought by moving over, I was going to create space for his buddy to sit up front with me. No. The whole idea was for me to exit. He wanted my wallet, he wanted my ring, he wanted me to empty my pockets. He wanted—and he got—everything. By that time, my mother had purchased a house on Long Island. I resided there with the rest of the family. After being robbed, I didn't have any money to take the Long Island Railroad home. I went to the police station, filed a stolen vehicle report, then asked the officers if they could spare me that $1.35 to buy a train ticket.

I never went back to driving a taxi. Truly, anyone who drives a taxi, especially in New York, let me tell you: you're basically taking your life in your hands.

My next jobs were much less dangerous. I worked at a bank, doing filing, and then I was promoted into the clearinghouse, and then to money transfers, foreign exchange, letters of credit, and ultimately audits. But in college I was studying to be a filmmaker. At that time in film history, that meant I'd have to go west. There was no Vancouver. No Tribeca Film Center. No Wilmington, North Carolina. My dream was to make it to California to see if I could be a cameraman. After seven years of going part time to school, after living at home, when I said I was departing, this was a real shock to some people.

Let me back up for a moment. My uncle Melcourt was the first of the family to immigrate—he was a great carpenter, and at that time, back in the fifties, America was looking for people to work. So my uncle ended up landing a job here. My grandmother used to come every winter to visit Melcourt, her son. After a while, Melcourt got married. Then my mom decided to come visit, and then in 1965, to immigrate for good. In 1964, my older sister Marie-Carle immigrated to Montreal, Canada. I was so upset. And my father was definitely upset. I missed my mother very much. You know, when you're still an adolescent, it doesn't matter if your parent punishes you, you still love that parent. Well, you wake up one day, and your parent is not around for you? Wow. You know? It was really truly a tough thing to deal with.

I wrote a letter to my mother. But my dad wanted to read the letter first, to make sure I spelled everything right, that the punctuation was perfect. He read the note and he said, "You're not going to send that letter." Because I was truly expressing myself, letting my mother know how unhappy I was that she left Haïti. Maybe my dad should have let me send that letter. Maybe my mother would have changed her mind and come back. I guess my dad wanted to protect her—I guess the words that I used were a little too harsh. So I never did send it.

My father arrived to America in March 1969. The next year, the other six of us kids came. This was the retinue for our arrival on August 18, 1970: me, Taylor, Michael, Alex, Richard, and Dannie—the name we all called Danielle. And then, in the end, here I am, coming to America, and I'm the guy representing my father! Doing things that my father wasn't doing for my mother. I was the guy driving. I was the guy taking my mother all around. I was the guy taking her to work, shopping, and everywhere else. Some guys I knew would say, "Oh, Georges is a mommy's boy." When I finally got married, on August 20, 1983, people said, "Georges got married?" They were shocked. I guess people thought that I was going to stay home and help out forever. But you know, I took a while, but once I graduated from college it was time for me to move on and do something for myself. So I left home and headed to California. That was in the early eighties. Soon, I got married, and in April of 1984, started my own business, the party rental business. The 1984 Olympics took place in Los Angeles and that was a boon for our then–brand new business—that summer, everyone was hosting events and needed tents and chairs and the like. Mostly, though, we sustained the business thanks to weddings, quinceañeras, retirement parties, municipal events—anything where people gathered.

I started the business in my garage with six hundred dollars. I opened up a bank account and borrowed against it. Every week I repaid the bank back twenty dollars. It was a form of discipline to try to establish credit. So I'd started my own business, and business started to go well. And time passed, and then, well, I ended up in a divorce. I ended up with two great kids. And I ended up running the rental business by myself, without my bilingual wife's help. And the business gradually was deteriorating, and I was distracted, and competition was starting to catch up to us. Dreaming of Haïti, dreaming of cuisine, dreaming of my family's past culinary enterprises, I said to myself, "You know what? I have to start something else."

ACRA

I F YOU GO TO somebody's house for a party and they
don't serve you acra, then you are definitely, truly
not at a Haïtian party.

Acra is the national dish of Haïti. You go
to a house party, you're going to be served acra. You
go to a street fair and you'll find acra. You attend a
carnival—acra.

On the menu it's spelled *a-c-r-a,* but it's pronounced
"accrats." I always thought that name came from West
Africa, from Ghana, where the capital city is Accra.
Charles Perry, the food critic who wrote one of the two
introductions to this book, told me that I'm incorrect.

He told me how Sierra Leone has *akara* and Nigeria has *akla*, and Ghana itself has fritters called *koose*. Thank you, Charles! I can say for certain that in Haïti, acra is consumed mainly in the southwest. My dad's family always prepared it, and he brought the recipe with him up to Port-de-Paix.

Acra is made from several ingredients: tarot root, green onion—the key element—and dry thyme. We also put egg yolk in there. And regular onion. Habanero chili. Black pepper. Parsley. And all this gets blended together. It's really a backbreaking food to make. First you gotta get some tarot root—I like ugly, older tarot. Then you've got to peel and hand grate it. Let me tell you: you gotta watch your fingers—you can easily scrape your hand. If you have nice-looking, expensive nails, don't risk them grating tarot.

Some people like acra with herring—I love it with herring! Some people like it with salted, dried catfish. And some people prefer black-eyed peas. At TiGeorges', naturally, we choose herring. After we've blended that mix together with the herring, we'll add a little bit of salt. Not much, since this is an ocean fish. By the way, I like to use almost the whole herring. I'll remove the head and everything else goes into the food processor. In Haïti, we never used a food processor. We would crush everything, okay? We would use a *pilon*, which is a wooden version of Mexico's mortar and pestle tools. But nowadays, I recommend the processor.

At first at my restaurant, people weren't ordering much acra. That's what I'd thought might happen—but Arlene, my ex-girlfriend, had been so convincing. So it's a lot of work, and it's such a great product. So I was doubly frustrated that people weren't enjoying it. I would sometimes give samples away for free and customers would just look at it and not eat it. Or they'd take a courtesy bite and say something like, "Oh, it's wonderful, but I'm very full." I thought long and hard about removing acra from the menu.

My son Benjamin loved to run the cash register. Loved to take orders. He and Michael were always squabbling over which one would take the orders, and which one had been more helpful that day. Michael would say, "Well, you didn't work enough." And Benjamin would reply, "No, Mike, you didn't work enough. I shouldn't be giving you too much of the tip." Michael would get mad. But anyway, none of us were selling much acra. But Benjamin's a big eater, and he said, "Well dad, if you're not selling it, I'm going to eat it." So Benjamin was the guy eating all the acra. Oh man! Let me tell you: that guy would really consume the stuff in big quantities! He was so enthusiastic that he became like our in-house advocate for acra. Customers would see this young guy, so passionately enjoying this strange dish. They'd ask him what he was eating, and next thing you know, they wanted a side order of their own. His endorsement really saved the day!

I don't know if it was all that attention he received, or something else, but soon enough Mike didn't want to work up front anymore. I said, "Michael, why don't you like to wait on the customers?" All he said was, "I want to be in the back."

This was around the time when I appeared on the Huell Howser show and business picked up. Michael would position himself near the back of the kitchen, on the steps to the rear entrance. I would say, "Michael, listen, I'm going to the bank," or to run some other errands. Michael would sit there, and about an hour later or two, I'd return. And Michael would tell me, "Hey dad, guess what? We sold twenty plates."

I was always wondering what Michael was doing back there. Turns out he was the man, really keeping his eyes on the business, monitoring everything, keeping tabs on the customers and the staff, and making sure people were not leaving through the back with the food. He was like the pit boss at a casino, or the foreman on a work crew. I was really impressed, and I was really thrilled. Mike and Ben cared about the business, and they really had my back, too. "You know," I thought, "I've created a good example for my kids." Mike, I'm happy. Trust me, you make me a very happy guy! Ben, the same for you! Oh, they are such good guys, my two boys.

I told you that when I was a kid, people in the neighborhood would piss me off, taunting me by calling me "Frenchie." Well, that doesn't happen to Mike and

Ben. But all three of us consistently face people not knowing where Haïti is located. People ask, "Where is Haïti? Where is that country at?" I'll say, "Well, it's near Cuba. We share an island with the Dominican Republic." The people will say, "Oh, are you Jamaican?" No! Haïti is Haïti, Jamaica is Jamaica.

For years, I've thought this is a big problem that I'm going to have to find a way to resolve. I'm patient with customers. I have maps on the wall. To no great avail, though. At home, in a closet, I had a Haïtian flag. I decided to bring it to TiGeorges' Chicken and fly that flag outside. The reason I had the flag was because there used to be a Haïtian guy by the name of Sebastien Vorbe playing for the Los Angeles Galaxy soccer club, and I used to take my kids to the games. We would go to the Rose Bowl, and we were like the only people supporting Vorbe. People wave their country flags at soccer matches, so I bought a Haïtian flag to go with the Salvadoran flags, the Mexican flags, the Brazilian. I said to Michael: "Hey, here's a flag, why don't you wrap it around yourself?" Mike said, "Well, I was not born in Haïti." But Benjamin said, "Michael, give me the flag." So Benjamin took the flag and wrapped himself. We stood near the spot where the players entered the playing field. Vorbe spotted us and he waved and clapped at the boys, who did it right back to him. It didn't take Michael much encouragement to feel that Haïtian spirit, whether he was born here or there! Also, we were all happy to support Vorbe. He was a fine player, but the

Galaxy rarely put him until the final ten or so minutes of a match. And we'd notice that whenever he got excited and started to push forward, the team always found a way to say, "Well, you out." I would say, "*Whoa whoa whoa*, the man is playing well. What's going on here?" Soon enough, alas, our lone Haïtian wasn't playing for the team anymore. I don't know what happened, because he is one of Haïti's best. He was as good as his dad. His dad was the one who took Haïti to the 1974 World Cup. That was the only time Haïti ever qualified to play for the Cup.

So, Vorbe's gone and there's no reason to bring the flag to games. I put the flag in our home closet. The Haïtian flag, you know, is derived from the French flag. After independence, we used the same colors from the French flag to make our own. When I thought to take that flag out of the closet and put it up front outside my restaurant, let me tell you: we're talking immediately about a true difference. This one white man walked into the restaurant and said, "Any man who would put the flag of his country in front of his restaurant must be proud of his cuisine, must be proud of himself, and must be proud of his homeland. Anything that you make here will be good. Sir, serve me."

Dramatic statement, huh? Well this guy, believe me, he really enjoyed the food. This was still early, and we didn't have a complete menu yet. He had the quarter chicken with rice and beans. I remember that man's sincerity and joy.

PIKLIZ

PIKLIZ. IT'S FUN TO spell, fun to say, and a hell of a lot of fun to eat.

In Haïti, we put pikliz on everything. We make a sandwich and put pikliz on that. Oh, that's another thing that my mother was good at: salami, cheese, and pikliz sandwiches.

For the Anglos, pikliz is a side dish, like pickles—which it sounds like but that's about it. For Salvadorans, it's like coleslaw that comes with a *pupusa*. To a Haïtian and those familiar with our culture, pikliz is pikliz: a yellow-colored combination of cabbage, lime juice, habanero chili, and carrots. Some chefs add onions, and some use sour oranges instead of the lime. My style, it's very basic: mix together key lime, salt, habanero chili, cabbage, and carrots. Add a touch of vinegar. Wonderful. Then sprinkle the pikliz on top of *tassot* and fried plantain, and we eat. People love pikliz, they can't get enough. Which is why TiGeorges' Chicken sells bottled pikliz. My brother Taylor back east packs the stuff. His packaging uses the business name, "Çeça." Out here, we use, "TiGeorges." Taylor's bottles and mine both feature the same photograph on the label: a shot of our grandmother.

The picture was taken by our brother Richard. Richard used to follow me around. When I was going to college to make movies, Richard was with me, carrying a cable. He took that photo of Suzanna Pierre during the final trip my grandmother made to America. She was sitting in the backyard of my mother's house on Long Island.

When you look at the photo, you see how, years ago, Haïtian women tied their hair. My grandmother's hair was white for as long as I can recall. She never wanted that known, though, so she used to cover her hair. She was young at heart, and I suppose wanted to camouflage her real age. So that's not a chef's hat she's wearing in the photo; that was just the style during the forties and fifties. It looks like high fashion, something you'd see in advanced society. My grandmother was a person with very little formal education, but when it came to fashion, let me tell you: she really studied. Come to think of it, you'd have to say that my grandmother was in the fashion industry. She used to supply ribbons to people, so they could decorate their wedding gowns and communion dresses. There were two people in our town who sold ribbons, and my grandmother was one of them. She'd go to Port-au-Prince and buy ribbons and yarn, too. She took the fashions that were in the capital and brought them to the province. She didn't know how to sew, but there was a seamstress school across the way and she'd have the students do her work.

My grandmother made sure I learned how to sew—the seamstresses taught me. My mother, though, couldn't make shirts. My mother would send us to the tailor, and he'd work his magic. We always wore clothing that was so nicely handmade. As a matter of fact, back then in Haïti, mass production didn't exist. You needed a pair of pants, you would go to the tailor and the guy would take a measurement and make something that fit you, and that endured.

On my restaurant's walls, I've hung up maps. I've got that photo, too, of my grandmother. And her again on the pikliz bottles. I've got a dozen framed articles about the restaurant from newspapers and magazines. I've got prints. And I've got more photos. One of those is, I think, the best photograph I've ever taken. It's of a man at the port, making rope. He's making that rope from disposed scraps that have washed to shore. The man would take those scraps by the ton to Port-de-Paix and weave them into longer ropes. Truly, this man had a talent. I found him by accident while I was trying to shoot a picture that would represent the Haïtian boat people. Because at the time, people kept saying to me, "Oh, Haïti? Boat people. Boat people. Boat people." It was like some sad mantra. The only thing you know about a place are images of people leaving? Terrible. I wanted to take a photo that would symbolize what Haïtians were more about, using that same imagery of the sea. I had this idea to capture a nice boat in port, empty, as opposed to a dilapidated jalopy of a boat, floundering at sea, overloaded with desperate people. To get the angle I wanted, I had to leave the pier and go into someone's backyard—and yes, I asked permission.

From almost behind a tree, I spotted this man, the rope maker. You see how he's looking away? That was typical then among Haïtians—people did not like to be photographed. Now, in this other photograph I took that's up on the restaurant wall, you see this mango merchant, out at an open-air market. She was quite uncommon, not just for her beauty and strength—which are typical of Haïtian women—but because she's looking straight into the camera. Aiming a camera at a Haïtian—that was a *no-no*. Most Haïtians didn't like it. This one woman, she was an exception. I saw her at a market in the north, while I was driving en route to the Citadel. That former military outpost is the eighth wonder of the world. It was the site where we fought the French in the late seventeen hundreds. I'd never been there, and I brought my camera to take some pictures.

On the way there, I figured, why not take some shots of the countryside?

By the side of the road, maybe an hour south of the Citadel, all these bright colors caught my eye. Orange and yellow and peach. All mangoes. I thought, "As a kid, I've seen all these different varieties of mangoes, but I've never tasted them." So I pulled over. The market spot was nice, in the shadow of a grove of trees. Very clean, very calm, very pleasant. Such an idyllic setting can make it easy to over-romanticize the hard life of an itinerant fruit vendor.

I started taking photos. Most of the other vendors were not too happy about this. But through my lens, I could see that far away, there was this lady kind of staging herself so she'd be part of the picture. Although I wasn't aiming at her at the time, she sort of composed herself into the frame. Well, I quickly gave her my full attention. I took a full roll of her. I didn't have to tell her anything, she was posing all along. When I got back to America, I developed the shots and let me tell you: she's absolutely beguiling. I made a print for her, and vowed to bring it back and let her have it as a small thank you. I haven't yet done that, and I suppose she might not still be around. But I'm certain someone else at that spot will tell me her whereabouts. That's how Haïti still is; people know each other.

Another thing about Haïti—people are still in pretty good physical shape. We don't have fast food chains on every block. We still eat well, and eat naturally. Rice, beans, mangoes. How old is the woman in my photograph? Her late twenties, I'd estimate. Look how strong she is, from transporting those mangoes in a straw bucket she places on her head. Those muscles don't mean she's not feminine! On the contrary, strong women are the backbone of Haïtian society. She's probably waking up at 2:00 a.m., then walking for three or four hours, carrying a heavy load. Then, six hours later, walking home. But then again, she might be older than I guessed. Haïtians hide their true age well. Maybe it's genetics, or pride like my white-haired grandma had. It's also that we stay fit by walking. If a person owns a bicycle, still, they'll walk. When I go to Haïti, I have a car at my disposal. But most of the time, I walk. That's how you get into conversations. That's how you find the best fritay. That's how you get the best feel for your countrymen and countrywomen.

Without a car, though, there'd be no photo of that mango merchant. And I'd never have made it to the Citadel. Of course, my muffler fell off twice during that trip—the roads were in such bad condition. And this was on the way to a leading tourist attraction! At another point, the battery cable disconnected. Hey, that's Haïti. Life's a mottled, bumpy road.

Oh, and life's full of honking. Another Haïtian cultural experience: if you're driving, you're expected to blare your car horn all the damn time. I have no idea why. Maybe it's considered festive. Maybe since Haïti is already a noisy environment, this is the only way to be heard. Maybe some cars are so old and broken down they don't have working horns, so it's a status symbol to bleat like a cranky, mechanical goat. Ten or so years ago, during one of my trips, I decided to experiment by not honking. Let me tell you: people were really upset with me. "Hey, Mister," I was told, "You have a horn in your car? Why don't you use it?" I guess other drivers always know where you are. Honking, it's like radar for Haïtians.

I mentioned how most towns have open-air markets that pop up one day each week. I used to go with my parents to one such market in a place called Chansolme. That market was open Tuesdays. It was about six kilometers from our house. You could find everything there. Goats. Mangoes. Rice. Beans. And also more car noise than a Formula 1 race. The market took place on the side of the main street, and so traffic would be blocked. People would just sit in their vehicles and honk, honk, honk. Like flocks of Canadian geese—I mean, if the geese didn't fly anywhere, but just kept their place in the sky. Very frustrating. C'mon, guys, the market happens every week. Let's either move the market away from the road, or build a diversion to the road a few kilometers prior. This is a solvable problem.

Open-air markets are really truly among my top memories of Haïtian life. Let's consider again that beautiful mango vendor. She has a straw bucket near her. Most likely, she carried the mangoes from where she lived. She would have filled that basket with mangoes and carried the basket for hours on her head. It's incredible to see. Some vendors bring their products on a donkey. Either way, these vendors are not getting rich. A bucket of mangoes used to cost me three or four cents. It's still incredibly cheap. That's in great part because Haïti produces so many mangoes, and we don't juice them, we don't freeze them, we don't do much of anything to extend the lifetime of the product. Once the mango harvest concludes, that's it, you're not going to find mangoes until next year. On one hand, this is an admirable commitment to consuming fresh and healthy seasonable crops. On the other hand, we've now got this beautiful woman, walking great distances carrying a bucket of mangoes on her head, to earn a few gourdes, and then the rest of the year, if you want a mango, you're out of luck. Another of my Haïtian dreams is to return and demonstrate to my former countrymen and women how to pack and store fruits. After the harvest, take steps to preserve some of the crop. Think about it, six months down the line, people would be able to purchase mango in a can or a jar. Sounds commonplace, right? No way, not in Haïti. I mean, local businesses don't have commercial freezers. That's one key reason why food has to be fresh, and why Haïtians are so suspicious of leftovers. People in Haïti will say, "Oh, did you make that dish this morning?" But in America, food preparation doesn't work that same way. In Haïti, if you expect maybe fifty people to come over, you're going to prepare food for fifty. Once supper's over, that's it. You don't have refrigeration, so you're not going to have leftovers. Here in America, people can show up anytime—at my house or at my restaurant—and instead of finding all the food sitting out on the stove, some of it will be preserved in the cooler or the freezer. If you can't come over today, no problem, we'll eat together tomorrow. Simple, right? Not in the old country.

Of course, there are great charms to the market culture. Going to market with my grandmother or my mother or my father may not have been an example of efficiency, but for a kid, it sure was enjoyable. Markets in the bigger cities would have hundreds of stalls, or *barks*, as we'd say in Kreyol. The bigger burghs would have a structure that would outline the market's boundaries— they'd call these structures *marché-an-fè*—a wrought- iron building. People would sell produce. Clothing. Milk. Sugarcane. Cocoa. Maybe a kite, vital to us kids. There'd be the meat section. The *abattoir*. There'd be lumber. Liquor. Flour. They'd be open all week, too. Again, this is only in the larger towns. Vendors would bring a piece of wood or two and lay them out as temporary tables, trying to make them not look lopsided. Occasionally, you'd find a guy who would make his bark look so nice, you could just tell this was a person who was going to take his business to the next level.

The open-air market was probably three blocks away from our house. That's where everybody—rich, poor, you name it—came together. That's the style of market that exists still in Haïti. The open-air market I'm talking about is from forty years ago. I'm not talking about the new Haïti. I'm talking about the Haïti that I knew, that had everything to make a country run. I remember when Haïti was really in order. We had the health department. We had the fire department. We had the tax collectors. We had all the establishments that would make a country run properly. Haïti had that. A neighbor of ours in Port-de-Paix, his name was Leon Legros, he was the health inspector. He used to go to the market with a gadget, and he'd check the milk that the vendors would be bringing down from the mountain. Some of the sellers would dilute the milk with water or some other liquids. They'd try to cheat you.

Leon Legros used to check this stuff out. If he determined that the milk had too much water, and wasn't really milk, he would trash it, right then and there. He'd pour that milk out. Us kids would go and see that bad milk flowing in the gutter, heading towards the ocean. Because this was not something that should be sold.

Watching Leon Legros work was among my favorite things to do. He'd carry a thermometer and check to see if the food was at the proper temperature. He'd check to see if the same products from the previous week were still on sale—if that was the case, let me tell you: Leon Legros was an iron fist. The man didn't fool around. Our town's market, you wouldn't get a bad batch. You wouldn't get sick. You wouldn't get cheated. And since everybody knows everybody else, even when the inspector was off duty, he was still that same guy. If somebody from the town sees him and complains, he'd go and investigate. You have a job like that, you're always working.

Truly, I learned my early lessons about health factors from this man. And then, when I arrive in America, I already know there are things that you simply just couldn't do in the kitchen. So my kitchen is clean, my cuisine is clean. It's a clean approach. You're not going to see food lying around in my kitchen. Food is in the cooler if it's not going to be served immediately. And if it's going to be served in an hour or two, it'll be in the warmer, ready to be served. My food is always fresh; I prepare dishes in small quantities. I don't fix large quantities, like mass production, where people would come and find food all the time. My motto is that it's better to say, "We don't have," versus giving customers a bad batch, a stale batch, a sick batch.

In the bigger cities, you'd smell the market before you saw it. But truly, the smell was acceptable to me. Because we had a sanitation department that cleaned everything up. You would see a lot of trash on the floor at certain times of the day, but once the market closed at 2:00 p.m. or 3:00 p.m., a cleaning crew came in to get it fresh for the next day. That's when the markets would close in the smaller areas as well. Once the market closes, the sellers pack up and head back to their homes. The peasants would go back to the mountain. And some of them would first stop at my mother's store. They would take some of their market earnings and buy things they couldn't get there—cake, bread and other bakery items, and rum, cola, and kerosene. Coming back from that market, they would make a pit stop right in front of my mother's house. Hers was the last store en route to the mountain. Most people were walking. Some people would be on donkeys, and some people would catch the bus. Well, it wasn't a bus, actually, it was something called a tap-tap. Which is very popular in Haïti, like an unlicensed taxicab.

Everybody worked at least five days weekly. Our family, it was six. On Sundays, except for my grandmother's squash soup concession, most things would shut down. People would head to church, then the beach. Here in Los Angeles, I do the same— Sundays, my restaurant is closed. Some customers complain—and I understand it's hard for everyone to make it here during weekdays. But remember, I'm also doing a cultural thing.

TiGeorges' Chicken is a Haïtian restaurant, and I like to send a message about how we do things in Haïti. Then again, restaurants in Haïti do open on Sundays for parties. Like if there's a first communion, a confirmation, a wedding, or a birthday. So I do the same thing here: if anybody wants to have a Sunday party, if you tell me two days prior, I'll be more than happy to open up for you!

PLÁTANOS FRITOS AND PLÁTANOS DULCES

'M BEGINNING TO FEEL a sense of fulfillment in my life.

In great part that's because of the restaurant. In 2007, I closed the party rentals business and expanded TiGeorges' Chicken. I expanded again in 2009. Now Los Puros has their own room to play in, and I can host seventy-five diners at once.

The greatest joy I get is still seeing people coming in and enjoying my food, complimenting me on the quality of my food, the taste and the flavor of my food.

So many of these people ask me, "What kind of spices do you use?" I tell them, "The same stuff that we all buy at the supermarket." What's different are our approaches, the way we use spices and other ingredients. Take plantains, for instance, which different cultures have different ways of preparing.

Sweet plantains are something I remember so well from my childhood. This was another item that vendors would sell every evening in the streets of Port-de-Paix. What a treat for us kids! The other day there was a lady eating at my restaurant, and she was telling me, "Well, Georges, my food never tasted this way. What do you do to make your sweet plantains so good?" I've come to find out that most people here fry their sweet plantains—their *plátanos dulces*—in chunks. That's not the best solution. Because chunks absorb the oil and you end up with a greasy mass of plantain. If you slice, not chunk, if you mince, then you'll end up with much less grease. That makes all the difference. Because the item's already so sweet, it has the tendency to absorb oil, which will render it tasteless. And not only that, but sliced and minced, the plantains will fry all the way through. If you're using chunks, the plantain's core will have a tendency to stay raw, since you'll be focused on not overcooking the visible exterior. Well, if you cook your plantains nice and slow, then the heat will absorb more evenly, and you won't wind up having too much fat or too much grease. I'm saying all this, again, because of taste. I'm not trying to prepare a healthy item here! In fact, I put brown sugar or caramel on top of my cooked plantain. This is what really truly enhances the taste.

Here's an interesting thing again about plátanos dulces: In Haïti, when we cut the plantain from the tree, the plantain is always green. We start consuming it green, but if we wait, then it becomes yellow—meaning sweet plantains. So if you walk into a Haïtian restaurant and ask for sweet plantain, you might not find one. It depends on the day.

Sweet plantains are yellow. Fried plantains are green. In Haïti, food is very colorful. I should put it like this: in Haïti, food *has to be* very colorful. I've seen people there refuse to consume food for a particular reason: lack of color. Why? Maybe because we Haïtians are delicate, or maybe we believe in eating foods that are really truly well-presented. Yes, color, and yes, aroma. These are the principles that really count in the Haïtian cuisine. Not only in my style of cooking, but in nearly every Haïtian household.

At my restaurant, I serve both plátanos dulces, the dessert, and plátanos fritos, the side dish. The latter is also part of our signature "The Island Combo" plate, along with rice and beans, salad, pikliz, and acra. When I think of plátanos fritos, I make so many wonderful associations. I know that the name alone of this dish appeals to many of my Latino customers. Because many

Latins love plátanos fritos. But it is also a Haïtian thing! We can eat it the green way and we can also eat it the yellow way. In Latin America, most people consume it yellow and sweet. But in Haïti, we mostly go green.

Preparing plátanos fritos isn't all that difficult. First, remove the green skin. Then dice your plantain into four or five sections. Then fry. Keep in mind that the plantain will sink to the bottom of the fryer. Once the food floats, then it's cooked. Take the plantain out, let it sit and set for a moment. Then squeeze it together. You can use two plates to do this, or a couple pieces of wood. Whatever works. Next, dip the plantain into slightly salted water. Finally, return the food to the fryer and have a quick go again, flipping equally between the two sides. Now, eat and enjoy! You can eat plátanos fritos with chicken. With fish. With griot. With the timalis sauce. With pikliz. The sky's the limit, okay? Green plantains are just like bread for the Haïtians.

Speaking of which, customers will occasionally ask me for bread. But you know something? Although my mother had a bakery, I don't recall seeing bread on our lunch or dinner table, only for breakfast or during the Christmas season. Bread was considered bad for us— too much starch. So when you come to my restaurant, considered yourself forewarned. No bread.

Every culture has its culinary customs—like the tortilla for Latin Americans, French fries for America, and bread for the French. Until recently, I wouldn't have known about Japan's culinary customs. But back in 2005, a Japanese restaurant owner invited me to his country to meet with him, cook for him, and discuss the possibility of collaborating. This man owns ten Haïtian-themed cafes located throughout Japan!

So I went for a week to Japan—specifically, to Tokyo and Yokohama. My good friend Stacy gave me the grand tour. She was the person who brought the restaurateur to my attention—who would have guessed that there are Haïtian eateries in Japan? Not me. Stacy teaches English over there, and when I visited, she really treated me great. Thank you, Stacy!

I found Japan to be, truly, an intimidating place. That was in part because of the language issue—if you don't speak Japanese, it's very difficult. Many people say they speak English, but in my experience, their vocabulary is limited to about twenty or thirty words. French and Spanish didn't help much, either. Kreyol? That would have been something, huh? I didn't dare try. So getting around would have been incredibly confusing if not for Stacy. Public transportation is incredible, but also can be technologically confusing and again, intimidating at some of these gigantic stations. Taxis were a disaster—so expensive, and so little English, and I've come to find out later, street names and mapping aren't so simple in Japan as they are here in the United States.

Those were the minor negatives, or minor obstacles. But fortunately, like people say, food is an international language. And when I walked into that first Haïtian café—the chain is called Café Haïti—truly you could forget you were in Asia. The presentation, the décor, the ambience—*oh, wow*. Let me tell you: the owner of the cafes went to Haïti and took back the best stuff, the real stuff, to display. I was impressed.

Before I departed Los Angeles, I told the owner of the Japanese cafes that I was going to cook for him, to really demonstrate to him what Haïtian food is all about. He was excited, and we met up at his café in Yokohama, which was a quick train ride from Tokyo.

The café was located inside a high-rise. The eatery had these well-finished, high glass walls with polyurethane wooden frames. It was very nice, and of course, very small. Somehow, they made the capacity to seat forty or fifty people. How they managed, I'll never know. They utilized every little spot you could imagine. And the people who work there and who eat there, they all understand. This is Japan. That's how it goes.

The café's walls were decorated with Haïtian artworks. They had some stuff made from steel drums and some colorful paintings. They had relics from huts and they had old photos. It was really nice. I was flattered to see how someone not in my culture would care to represent my culture at that level. I give them a "ten."

Ambience is nice, certainly, but taste matters more. I was so excited to cook for this man and his associates. I brought much of what I needed from Los Angeles. I cooked lambi for him, which I brought frozen in a dry ice bag. I brought habanero chili, thyme, key lime—

basically, the most vital ingredients I was going to need, and that I didn't trust I could locate over there. I even brought paprika. My guy told me I'd find paprika in Japan, but I wasn't confident—I mean, there's little use for that spice in the local cuisine. I told him I wanted to make herring, and he told me, "No problem." Well, I didn't find any herring, but I found something similar: a hard, dry fish, something you had to chew on like a jerk piece. I soaked that fish in water, let it sit there to see how much I could weaken it. That turned out okay. I took out my tarot root and peeled it and grated it. The chef at the café, he really wanted to do this too. He ended up scraping his finger and required a Band-Aid. But no matter, the chef was happy! To him, this was something new, something exciting, something he was pleased to be participating in. So, I proceeded. I mixed the ingredients to do the acra. I'd gone to the supermarket that morning to get green onions and bell peppers—*whoa*, extremely expensive! For a single bell pepper, I paid three dollars. Anyway, I showed the owner and the cook how to make the acra and then how to preserve the acra so it will stay good later. With the very little English that he spoke, the chef made it clear to me he wanted his turn. "Move to the side, Georges," I think he said. "I'm gonna show you."

So the guy went ahead and made the acra, and they were shaped exactly right. The guy was watching me, truly observing me on every level. And he delivered quality.

The café's food—excellent as it is—is still not totally typical Haïtian cuisine. The stuff on their menu all came with an Asian accent. When Haïtians make squash soup, we use bone marrow to create the base. We put vegetables in, like carrots and potatoes. In Japan, though, it's more of a puree with soy sauce. Very good, but that Asian texture comes through every bit as identifiable as the Haïtian.

That's what made the owner and the chef and everyone else go crazy for the timalis sauce I prepared. Oh my goodness! This was a revelation. They couldn't believe this taste. Even the owner's wife joined us. That's something Japanese don't always do, bring their wives in to a thing like this. From what I witnessed, often the wives stay on the side, not participating in social activities. This was a strong message that I was truly welcome, for him to bring along his wife. And it was great news that she wanted to find out how I cooked. She didn't speak a word of English, but I'm sure she had plenty of positive things to say, because of the expressiveness in her face. She ate my food, and then kept going for more. And all the other workers at the café were there, too, and everyone indicated they enjoyed the meal.

I started them all off with acra and timalis. Then, rice and beans. Haïtian rice and beans are different from the usual Asian white rice—using the local stuff, I wasn't able to one-hundred-percent replicate my restaurant's flavor, which was disappointing. Lastly, I prepared the lambi. The owner asked me a million questions. "What is this, Georges?" I had to explain to him, it's a shellfish. It's a cousin of oyster, clam, and abalone. Let me tell you: this was a big hit, there was no lambi left. Everyone who was there in that restaurant that day tasted it. Some of them were a little bit reluctant—I can understand that because it was something foreign. But once they tasted it, they said, "Holy cow! This is good!" They ate and had fun. Drinking was another big thing. We're at the table and all I hear is: "Georges, one more drink. Another drink. Another drink." Hey, I was prepared. I kept drinking. All the workers were drinking. That's something I don't always see here in America—workers sitting at a table with the owner, with the principle of an operation, enjoying beers together, everyone going to the fountain and serving himself another. And another. And another. I guess that's the norm. I went to other restaurants, eating late at night, and that's what I saw. That camaraderie was impressive.

After I finished cooking at Café Haïti, I presented my host with my chef's apron and my monogrammed chef's shirt. He loved them both. He donned them and I took a photograph. We were both so happy—me, experiencing Japan. And him, able to demonstrate to his workers and his customers that here is TiGeorges, from Haïti by way of Los Angeles, preparing a meal in one of his kitchens. After I returned to the United States, he and I continued to exchange emails. I haven't made it back to Japan since, but I really do look forward to that day.

Oh, by the way, people have asked me, "What's it like watching Japanese people eat Haïtian cuisine?" Yes, they use chopsticks. They give you a spoon with the chopsticks, no fork, no knives. And of course, at the restaurant, everything is small. Not just the dining room, not just the kitchen, but the plates and the food— everything is served in small portions. You can have as much as you want, though. Even if you go to a buffet, everything will be small portions.

Did I learn anything on that trip about cooking that I can bring to my restaurant? Not really. The thing that most turned me on in Japan was the sense of discipline and punctuality. When I say to people that I felt at home in Japan, it's because I'm a very punctual person. When I say ten o'clock, I'm a guy that will be there prior to ten. For a Japanese person, in my experience in that nation, being on-time means being half an hour early. Coming late is a huge *no-no* in that culture. Everybody is always running. When I was there, I thought, "Why don't the Japanese win all the marathons?" Because everybody is always running to the train, even though there is another one coming in about five minutes. Why would the guy want to run and almost break a leg to catch that train? It's that sense of discipline, the sense of being punctual. Timeliness is not something that the Japanese take for granted.

You know, I did enjoy eating over there, too. I just didn't learn any techniques for my restaurant. I had this one lunch at Shinjuku—that's the world's busiest train station, I think. I went there and wandered around at this incredible, massive intersection with all these monumental electronic screens with advertisements playing. It was like Times Square times twenty! This was my last day in Tokyo, and it was mid-morning. Restaurants don't open for lunch until 11:30 a.m., so I wandered and waited. When I found a place, let me tell you: what an incredible meal! They started me off with miso soup and rice—of course, you're in Asia, you're almost required to have white rice. Then they brought out the *shabu shabu*. Oh, yes! Shabu shabu! If you go to Japan, you've got to do this. If you don't already know, shabu shabu is a style where you cook your own food. They gave me vegetables, I cooked them right there. They gave me an egg, and I thought they wanted me to consume it raw, which I wasn't about to do. But of course, I was supposed to cook that egg in the same gravy, the same sauce, where the vegetables were cooking. I rolled it around in that roiling sauce, cooked it properly, then I removed the shell and ate it.

When you visit another culture's institutions, it's important at least that first time to pay proper respect and take part in customs that will, literally, be foreign to you.

I've eaten Korean meals where they bring out a boiling clay pot full of stew and expect you to crack an egg and drip it into the stew. I've been to health food places, particularly twenty-five years ago, where they expected you to drink a raw egg mixed with protein powder. In any of these cases, if you refuse, the people around you, the people who operate the premises, they'll be thinking, "Hey, who are you, man, to defame my culture?"

Like in my restaurant, every now and then, a well-meaning customer will bring in tortillas. I know how that makes me feel. Tortillas—they are not part of the Haïtian culture. They are excellent, and they work well with meals designed for them. But please, guys, *no más tortillas.*

Over the years, I've been fortunate to travel to a few other places, in addition to Japan. I know three-quarters of South America and three-quarters of the United States. I know part of Canada, and the Caribbean. I went to Hong Kong—which I'd always wanted to do because of the great movies shot there. I've been to Singapore— great cuisine, where East meets West. Hong Kong, too, has great cuisine. Japan has great cuisine, but expensive. If you travel to Japan, then you better have some money in your pocket. But in Singapore, you're going to enjoy some great seafood for an inexpensive price. For fifteen Hong Kong dollars, which is like eight US dollars, in Singapore you're gonna enjoy some lobster, some shrimp, and best of all, some Tiger beer.

Where else have I been? How about Bolivia and Honduras? In Bolivia, they serve something close to what the Argentineans do, blood sausages. That's something that we also do in Haïti, we call it *boudin*. When I was in college, I visited Bolivia. I bumped into two guys on the plane who were about my same age. They were definitely from rich families. When I got to Bolivia, I didn't have to spend a cent. I was invited to stay at their houses, invited to eat dinner out every night. It was truly a wonderful experience. They took me that first night to a hotel where I ate truly Bolivian food. This was a meal that remains in my mind today. Watercress served with blood sausages, then shallots marinated in vinegar. Let me tell you: *excellent, excellent, excellent*!

In Honduras, I visited the Mayan ruins in the city of Copan. This is a famous and important location for anyone who is a descendant of the Latin world. The ruins were amazing. So, though, was the meal I ate right there. I had unbelievable, and familiar, chicken. What made that meal so great were the spices, which are similar to what we use in Haïti. The taste was eighty-five to ninety percent similar to Haïtian cuisine. The gravy, the way the chicken was cut—they basically do it just the way I do. They separate the white meat from the dark. They add onions. One of the few differences was the way they incorporated a little bit of carrot. That overall taste, I'll never forget. And the meal was very inexpensive. I think lunch cost forty or fifty *lempira*, which was probably three to four US dollars. It was really cheap and it was great food.

There are so many great world cuisines—and so many more I'd like to experience, particularly in Europe. I've been asked, "If you were going to open up another restaurant—not serving Haïtian food—what would you do?" That's easy. Italian. Definitely Italian. My favorite world cuisine is Italian food. I love white clam sauce with linguini! Lasagna! And of course, pizza. When we were living in Brooklyn, on Eastern Parkway, in 1970, hey, there were so many Italian restaurants! So coming to America, that was the food that we could really truly enjoy. Meatloaf, it wasn't something that I wanted. Pot roast, I didn't know what to make of that, it seemed to be so extreme, so lacking in the kinds of flavors I was used to. But when you'd go to an Italian restaurant, you would see garlic, you'd see oregano, you'd see tomato paste and sauce. That's probably why I so quickly embraced the Italian cuisine. So much of it is familiar to a Haïtian palette. And the rest of it? I'm a quick learner when it comes to great food.

Oh, by the way, at my restaurant, I offer one menu item that's not Haïtian, just in case someone comes with a group for a function or something and just can't abide our cuisine. What's that one alternative item? Chicken linguini. *Buon appetito!*

DRINKS AND DESSERT

COFFEE, RUM, AND COLA

MY FATHER, FOR A brief period of time, was Haïti's director of customs.

I guess he got fired. Or at least, one day he just no longer had the job. Because you know when you hold a government position, and a new political party takes charge, then, well, you no longer hold that position. That happens in most countries. That happened to my dad.

When he was customs director—this was back in the fifties—Haïti's main exports were coffee, cacao, and another commodity called *danre mascriti*. This is a seed that produces synthetic oils, and Haïti was also a great producer of that at the time.

I used to love going to visit my dad's office. But once he lost his job, he had to start over. But he had some money, and he had connections with all the big companies that were shipping products to Europe. So these guys would give my dad money to go buy coffee for them.

That's how my dad ended up going into the deepest parts of the mountains of Haïti. He bought some property by a riverbed, right in the heart of other coffee plantations. It was truly an intense business because people expected him to deliver more than he could. On occasion, we would have rain, and that would make it very difficult to dry coffee. And of course, there was always competition, people who were buying at a much higher price than he could offer.

My dad was always independent, and he was able to get the beans before his competition. Why? Because he went places where most Haïtians—and definitely most Europeans—wouldn't go. He lived with the mountain peasants five nights per week. It wasn't the greatest of conditions. Usually, he slept on the floor. And that nearby river, it wasn't too far from the ocean. And when that river flooded, it was like watching the Colorado River rapids. That's how mean that river could be! It messed with anything in its path—cars, animals, people, whatever got stuck in the mud and sand and roaring water. So here was my dad, with a nice home in Port-de-Paix, but for more than a decade, from the late fifties through the late sixties, he's sleeping on the floor, in the mountains, being a true coffee speculator. Looking at it today, he was truly a special man to make the decision to do all of that. I've mentioned how some educated Haïtians do not want to plant trees or cook a fish. Yes, I do criticize Haïtians for that—but not my father. He set an example to be followed.

The place where my dad bought property and went to live is called Anse a Faleur. We all loved going there—it was a great place for a vacation. It took the family about five hours to get there from Port-de-Paix, because of the bumpy, sometimes barely passable roads. And, we were in the pickup truck, which my dad drove very slowly—he wanted to protect that truck and protect us kids, too.

It hadn't always been possible to drive to his place. Previously, you could walk or ride a donkey. My dad had a road built so he could bring his truck in to pick up the coffee loads. He'd bring the goods back to the city every Saturday. I'd stand on the sidewalk near our house at around 1:00 p.m., waiting for his truck to make that turn into view.

Dad would usually spend Saturday and Sunday selling, go to the bank Monday morning, and then head back to the mountains. We lived across from the bank—again, everything was convenient. Coffee was a cash business, and people would bring my dad bags of money. I chased my dad wherever he went. My dad would turn to me and say, "Oh, why don't you hang on to this bag of money." I remember, when I was seven years old, my dad handing me bags with hundreds and hundreds of gourdes. And at that time, the currency of Haïti was equal to the dollar of the United States of America. So that was a lot of money! I would keep that money bedside. On occasion, I would take a dollar or two. And my dad never recounted that money. That's how much my dad trusted me. I suppose I didn't completely reward that trust!

What would I do with that dollar? Usually, I would invite my friends and we'd go eat. Maybe get some fritay, or something else we couldn't get at home. My mother's bakery and store were known for many things, including selling the best sandwiches. In our part of Haïti, you wanted cold cuts, my house was the only place to get that. My parents used to go buy Swiss cheese, mustards, and Italian products like salami. If you wanted to eat something that wasn't in the Haïtian culture, my family had that.

So, my mom had the bakery and now my dad was in the coffee business. Seems like a perfect food marriage, right? Here in LA, of course, TiGeorges' Chicken serves Haïtian coffee. But originally, I used a local Los Angeles coffee supplier. One week, the guy was unable to deliver. So, I called home and I spoke with my mother. She was eighty-five years old then, still healthy. I told her, "Ma, this gentleman used to sell me my coffee and now I'm unable to get it." My mom said, "What you talkin' about? I can send you coffee."

So since that call, I basically do coffee in my restaurant in the same fashion that my dad prepared it in Haïti. I serve Blue Mountain coffee that comes from the environment where I grew up. What makes the coffee of Haïti so special? The environment. Especially where my dad used to cultivate, at an elevation. The weather is really cool at night, just the right temperature to make great coffee. And in Haïti, we basically use no pesticides, no chemicals—there's no great rush to market—so the beans grow naturally.

People tell me that Blue Mountain coffee comes from other islands, other nations. Actually, Blue Mountain coffee is from—Haïti! The translated meaning of Haïti is "mountainous." When you traverse Haïti, you are either going up or you are going down. Coffee grows in elevation, four thousand feet or so. And the temperature drops from one hundred degrees with high humidity during the day to like forty degrees at night. This is the ecological recipe that produces a great quality of coffee.

In my family—and probably in yours, too—coffee was essential to our lives. We didn't have a clock or a rooster to wake us up in the morning. Our neighbors would be percolating coffee. Let me tell you: that's the best wake-up call! Today, in Los Angeles, I visit various coffeehouses and something crucial is missing: aroma. I ask myself, "Are they adding some flavor to give this coffee taste?" Because there's a certain way coffee smells.

In Haïti, we do not need to add anything to achieve this flavor. Coffee is natural. We don't use fertilizer, we don't use pesticides. We don't have big farms like they do in Central and South America. Everyone who owns a piece of land in the mountains of Haïti, they cultivate coffee. When you work on an intimate scale, quality is more easily controlled.

Making coffee is a complex process. When you remove the cherry part of the bean, you don't wash it immediately. You let it stay in a vat for three or four days to ferment, and to slough off the gluey part of the bean. My dad would buy beans on Monday, then take them out of the vat toward the end of the week. Then he'd use this machine that resembles a small plough and remove the first skin—coffee beans have a couple of skins. In French, this process is called *decortiquer*.

After the fermenting, you wash and then dry the beans. This isn't as straightforward as it might seem. Coffee harvest happens during the rainy season. Drying requires sun. You might have a daily window of three sunny hours—but that's not enough. The rains would often happen in the late morning, so you'd start at 6:00 a.m., pouring the coffee out on the concrete pavement. When you'd hear thunder, you'd bag up the coffee and bring it inside the warehouse. It's funny—back then I thought of my dad's tiny, windowless shed as being a warehouse. I mean, it was made of mud and straw. A warehouse? I'd never seen a Costco back then!

Once the weather broke long enough and the beans dried, then it'd be time to remove the second skin. That gets you to the green coffee, this fiber stays in there until you roast the beans. That great coffee aroma we're so accustomed to? Let me tell you: at this point in the operation, it's a rotten smell! By day three, though, that great smell starts to come through. When it does, people get excited. That means good taste, and good profit. The workers gather for a harvest party—we call it a *conbit*. A goat or other animal is killed and prepared, a big banquet is held.

At TiGeorges' Chicken, I keep a photograph in the hallway that displays my father's coffee property. The shot shows that "warehouse"—or hut—and it also shows a bunch of young kids playing around. Those are the grandchildren of some of the people who worked for my dad. I went back in 1983 to visit the plantation. I made contact with people who used to work for my dad, as well as with some of his old competitors. I met the workers' families. Many people gave me their names, so I could keep a historical record. And so that when the time comes, I can contact them again to restart the operation. I'm working on that, and by the time you read this book, ask me if the Laguerres are once again in the Haïtian coffee business. Because going there, I felt duty-bound to bring the grounds back to life, restore the enterprise, help the local economy, and yes, honor my father's legacy.

During that same 1983 trip, I was also scouting for a location to perhaps get into the wine-making business. I haven't done that yet. Haïti has the weather conditions and the elevation to make great wine. Back around the eighteen hundreds, a volcano erupted in Mexico, and ashes were deposited in Haïti's Northwest. That soil addition is one reason why that area produces citrus. The elevation and proximity to the sea helps, too. These are the same factors that exist in Napa Valley. Before my trip to Haïti, I went up to Napa and talked to people there about my vision. One guy trusted me with five hundred vine cuts—French *colombard*. I brought them to Haïti and when I got there everybody was so happy to see me. But operating a vineyard didn't come close to working out, because the people my family knew from the coffee business didn't know anything about wine or about cultivating grapes. But above all, it was me. I wasn't ready. I didn't have enough money. I needed a lot more land than what my father left me. To make a profit, I'll need to purchase more. Don't count me out. Don't count Haïti out. The place could be the next Bordeaux.

Back then, and still today, wine isn't Haïti's alcoholic drink of choice. Neither is beer. When comes to boozing in Haïti, we're talking rum—sugarcane rum.

In the United States, of course, it's forbidden for fourteen year olds to drink hard liquor. But I'm sure it happens behind closed doors. In Haïti, it was okay; we'd drink in front of our parents. It wasn't a no-no. I don't ever recall my mother saying not to drink. As a matter of fact, because my mother sold rum at her store, my brothers and I would get to do taste tests. The rum would come by the truckload, in 150-gallon barrels. Thirty or forty of those barrels would arrive every week or two. Some unscrupulous sellers would water the rum down, so we'd do some quality-control work. We'd taste it, yes, but we'd also check for wax buildup. The wax comes from within the liquor itself—there's something in the cane that produces wax. Once the rum settles in the barrel, the wax separates. My brother Eddie and I would check to make sure there was the approximate usual amount of wax—less wax would mean more water or some substance that wasn't rum. Eddie and I would collect all the wax and make candles. My mother, meanwhile—provided the rum was good—would turn around and sell the drink in smaller quantities. People would come to the store with one-gallon or five-gallon containers. This was a lucrative part of her business.

The rum barrels were too bulky to fit inside the store, so they'd be out in our yard. My brother Taylor loved to hide behind those barrels! If you were seeking out Taylor, the best place to check would be behind a barrel. And he'd probably be eating ketchup or tomato paste. You simply couldn't keep enough of that stuff around! Anyway, Taylor would be hiding out, eating tomato products, and then he'd fall asleep in the midday heat. Meanwhile, my brothers Eddie and Michael and I liked to drink rum, and we liked to experiment making our own flavors of booze. We'd take some rum, mix in pineapple skin and see if we could make cognac or something similar. We'd seal up our bottle and bury it for a month. We'd await fermentation, dig up the bottle, and take a whiff of the aroma. Smelled good? Then we'd try it. Our stash would often turn out pretty good—or at least that's what a trio of us teenage boys thought. The true expert in town was a woman named Sofina. She would come buy rum from my mother and then she'd take the goods to the next level. She'd collect certain roots—she kept the recipe secret—and she'd mix them together. She'd add a bit of sugar and let the concoction age. Let me tell you: that drink was incredible, both sweet and substantial. People in Port-de-Paix to this day will ask their bartender for a "Sofina." Everyone's got a different version of what this means.

I mentioned earlier how I was drinking rum as a teenager. Let me tell you: I had my first cup of Haïtian coffee when I was two years old. A maid served it to me, diluted with water and not scalding hot. I drank that variation of coffee for years. In fact, watered-down warm coffee remained my brother Alex's favorite drink for years. Hey, for all I know, maybe Starbucks sells this stuff under a funny name and at a high price.

TiGeorges' Chicken doesn't serve rum, and most certainly we don't serve watered-down coffee—unless Alex wants to come by and make a special order. For you, my brother, I'll do it! What we do serve, and what customers really truly seem to love is Cola Lacaye, Haïtian soda. When people taste this cola, they say,

"What is this?" Well, it's natural fruit syrup with carbonated water. We carry a banana flavor, a fruit cola, and a cola champagne. Here in America, we're accustomed to dealing with caffeine, like what's in Pepsi and Coke. But in Haïti, soda pop doesn't have caffeine, it's naturally made. But because people are so accustomed to the American style, when they come across Haïtian cola, they'll say things like, "Hmm, what is it? It tastes like bubble gum."

What I normally say to people, if you really want to bring back tastes from childhood, then try the Haïtian cola. And guess what? The colas I serve in my restaurant? When I was growing up, the distributor's family was my family's business competitor. The distributor, his name is Rigobert. We were friends in Haïti, and we remain friends in America, we do business together and look out for one another. Rigobert's dad used to have a bakery, like my mom's. Now I'm selling Rigobert's product. The only request I make of my old friend is to bring more banana—that's the most popular flavor at my restaurant.

Now, please forgive me a moment. For those of you who have ever lost someone, I believe you'll understand the following. For no particular reason, writing up above about Rigobert and Haïti, I was just absolutely overwhelmed with memories of my brother Eddie. Eddie's no longer with us. He spent much of his life in ill health. He returned to Haïti and died at the young age of forty-two. I miss Eddie very much. He contributed so much to the success of my life, and to my restaurant.

The lessons Eddie taught me extend even to the decoration of my restaurant. We painted some of the walls here the color of Cola Lacaye's champagne flavor, a soft orangey hue. Customers ask me, "How did this color come about?"

The colors of all the walls came naturally, to some extent, and then again, also by accident. That's part of art—the mind is constantly creating, looking for something new and different.

I was rushing to leave for a visit to New York, not knowing how I should paint this place. The night prior, I went to Home Depot and got the paint. My cousin was doing the work and the next day he tells me I didn't get enough. I said, "Let's improvise. Let's mix this color with that color, and that color with that other color."

This is typical in Haïti. There's always a shortage of something. You would go to the store, try to buy paint, and maybe the guy would only have two gallons. So here you are, going home with the intentions of doing something grandiose, and you get started and then you run out of paint. So you go back to the paint store and see if more of that color has arrived or been made. Usually, the answer was no. So, you figure something out. The same thing goes for the restaurant. We run out of food, and I'll improvise something. I'll make a fresh batch of something. If you happen to arrive at TiGeorges' and we've just run out of what you're ordering, then I guarantee you're going to end up with something great. Things that maybe I couldn't make a full dish with, maybe a mix of things.

This is something that I learned from Eddie. When I used to work with him during summers, sometimes he would be asked to prepare food for five hundred people. And let's say three hundred wound up eating. That left good food for two hundred. Eddie would put that all in the cooler, and the next day, he'd refresh it. He'd invent a new dish with the leftovers—these would often be the best of the best, the most flavorful and the most innovative ideas. This is even more startling considering that in Haïti people don't like leftovers.

Haïtian ex-pats will come to my restaurant and ask me, "Is this food fresh?" What do you mean, is it fresh? Of course it is fresh! My restaurant food—I don't use any preservatives. When I put food in the cooler, it stays there. If it's in the freezer, it stays there, and usually in a small quantity, sufficient for two or three days.

Haïtians think that if something has been in the refrigerator or the freezer, then it is not considered fresh. Well, I got news for you guys: this is the modern world, this is how it's done. Everything is prepared and put away in the freezer, man. That's how you're going to keep the food fresh, that's how you're going to prevent bacteria from invading the food. You cook food and then you let it sit on the stove? You better sell it and serve it fast. If it sits there for over an hour or two, you're definitely gonna have to trash that food. It is much more dangerous to keep your food out there, thinking it's gonna be the fresher product. If your food has been cooked, put it away in the cooler or the freezer. When it's time to serve, reprepare it. This is the healthier approach. Sorry, Haïti.

I just had another memory pop up to remind me of Eddie. One time Eddie took me to eat at a seafood joint in Baltimore—this was when he was making good money working at the country club.

He ordered me oysters with boiled eggs. I said, "*Hmm*?" I was asking him, "How do you eat this?" Eddie said, "Slice the egg and put it on top of the oyster, then put on your Tabasco or your oyster sauce, whatever, and then slurp the whole thing down." Let me tell you: this was *gooood*. You better believe I enjoyed it. I'm laughing here thinking about what the expression on my face must have been that day—boiled eggs and oysters are not Haïtian foods. I'm laughing and I'm thinking about Eddie.

Eddie always told me, "Your place must be clean. You must always give people good food. And if a customer comes to your restaurant and doesn't enjoy his meal, then you have to find out if there's any other way to please the customer." And when people see me at work, they say, "Well, Georges is always talking." People say, "Georges, how do you get so much energy? How do you manage?" It's because I enjoy what I do. And because I was taught by the best: By my grandmother. By my mother. And by Eddie.

PAIN PATATE

PAIN PATATE IS A white yam that can be found in the Caribbean and the Pacific Island Asian countries, South America, or Central America.

Yams and sweet potatoes are central to Haïtian life. There's a proverb that says, *"Nan tan grangou patate pa gen po"*—basically, during times of famine, eat the potato's skin. Like I keep saying, we Haïtians are resourceful, and we are survivors.

Here, though, we are about to speak about luxury— not just survival. We talking about dessert—the farthest food distance from famine. We're talking about sweet potato pudding. One of the great codas to a TiGeorges' Chicken meal.

Let me tell you: as kids, we'd leave for school early in the morning, and before class, we'd seek out this lady, this merchant, who used to sell pain patate. We simply couldn't go to class without eating this stuff early in the morning. It's so great to eat, but it requires a lot of effort to make. First of all, you'll need the white yam, not the orange yam we use at Thanksgiving. This yam is found in tropical environments. I find mine in LA at an Asian market. Central American or Caribbean groceries carry them, too.

Now, wash that yam, because usually there's a lot of dirt on it, okay? Wash thoroughly. Then peel off the skin and grate. Back in Haïti, we'd find dry coconut and we'd grate that, also. But here in America, these things come pre-prepared. So, pick up a can of grated coconut—it usually comes in a syrup. Now add a quarter pound of grated ginger. Next, add key lime skin. Make sure it's green so you encounter the flavor you're looking for. Then grate some nutmeg. And put essence in—vanilla. And a little bit of salt. Mix it all together, add some evaporated or concentrated milk. Next, take two or three pounds of bananas—they've got to be extremely ripe. In Haïti, we'd add some brown sugar, but here, there's no need because of the coconut syrup. By the way, coconuts in syrup and evaporated milk are the only items you'll find in my kitchen that come from cans. Otherwise, everything else is made from scratch.

Now, the mixture has to be cooked. Use a low fire and stir constantly. Blend in a little butter, so you get a little more fat in there than just from the coconut. You should be cooking with a big, heavy pot. If you possess little tiny pots that are not resistant to heat, don't use those because you're going to burn the yams. Depending on the intensity of the fire, you'll probably cook for about twenty-five minutes. You've got to stand by. You've got to pay attention. You cannot just leave the food there and run away. Good cooking requires attention. Good cooking, you got to stay present and focused. Good cooking, you can't say, "Okay, let it cook. I'll go tend to something else and come back later." *No no no no!* Keep stirring. Once the mix is golden brown, you're on your way to earning your just desserts. Get some butter or oil down at the bottom of the pot and put that pot in the oven at 350 degrees. When it's ready, you'll know. It'll smell so good. Take it out and let it cool off. I recommend waiting a day before you eat, to really let those flavors lock themselves together. But take as much time as you can. You might not be able or willing to resist. Last steps: add caramel or chocolate or some ice cream—vanilla preferably.

My pal Gabriel, he always has on hand the best Häagan-Dazs ice cream. But eventually, I'd like to find the time to make my own ice cream. For now, thanks, Gabriel, for the store-bought stuff. Gabriel and I became friends many years ago. He used to be a rocker. He was the guitar player in a band in Boston. When I was going to college, my good buddy Phillip and I used to travel to Boston, and I used to bump into Gabriel. Philip and Gabriel were dating two sisters. So we'd go to visit Philip's date and we'd also hang out with Gabriel and his date.

When I made it out to Los Angeles, it was harder to make friends. Particularly Haïtian-born friends. In New York, there were whole bunches of Haïtian people living there. LA—not so many. Early on, became pals with a guy called Tommy. He was the district manager of a fast food chicken chain. He knew how broke I was, and he knew about my cooking skills—not that I'd need them for what he was about to offer. Evans tells me, "Hey, Georges, I can get you a job."

Oh, man. Here I am, a recent college graduate, moved across the country to make it in Hollywood, but nothing's happening in that realm. I'm not getting any leads, I'm not making connections, and I'm definitely not getting any cameraman work. I've had my own business, driving a cab, and I've already worked at my mom's diner, and at Winston's, that fast food place, back east. So what in the world am I thinking when Evans offers me a gig? I'm thinking, "I'm broke." And I'm thinking, "Don't be so proud." I said to Evans, "Yes, thank you."

Evans set me up with an interview with a supervisor. I was living in Santa Monica with my uncle Abner. It turns out that fast food chicken chain job was supposed to go to someone truly needy. Now if you're a homeowner in Santa Monica, obviously you're not needy. The supervisor told me that if I could get a California ID showing a different address, then the job would be mine. I knew a guy in LA, on Union Street. I said to him, "Chito, I need to use your address." Chito said, "Yeah, go ahead."

So I went to the DMV and got a temporary residence card that said I was residing on Union, and then I went to the supervisor and got the job. "Yeah, yeah," I said to my family. "I'm selling fast food now." They weren't impressed—but they were pleased I was finally working again.

I don't want to put the chicken chain down because these places are what they are, and by working at them and eating their food, all of us who do that are complicit. But, still. Let me tell you: where I come from, we do not cook chicken in this manner. We want to know what's being put in our meals. We don't want some pre-prepared solution, some "secret" ingredient that's probably kept secret because of how embarrassing it'd be if revealed. And the cooking process this place used. Let me tell you: I mean, get a vat. Dump all the chicken parts in the vat. Get a hose. Fill the vat with water. Dump the solution in there. Let it marinate overnight. The next day, drain it, cut it, dip it in milk and butter, and then fry it. So much grease! For the meals I ate there, I'd wipe the chicken down and then add some spice. It didn't do much, but then again, I was poor and very hungry.

I mentioned earlier how my brother Taylor used to, as a kid, eat lots of ketchup and hide out behind the barrels of rum in our backyard. Guess what? That formula produced a wise and motivated man. Taylor came out to California to visit me, and he said, "Well, Georges, you've been out here long enough. If you're unable to get a decent job, it's because you're doing something wrong."

I said, "What do you mean, I'm doing something wrong?" But of course, he was correct, I was in denial. Taylor said to me, "Buy a *Los Angeles Times*, look in the 'Help Wanted' section. Find a better job." He opened up the paper, found a bookkeeping position open at a party supply business, and told me—demanded, really—that I call the place. I did, and thanks to my banking experience, I was hired on the spot by a fine man named Dick.

I did a good job, and I looked at the business like it was my own. One, because it was a black-owned business. And two, because the place needed that extra bit of help. My job was bookkeeping. But when the place was dirty, I'd go to the drug store and buy cleaning solution. I'd be well shaven. I'd be wearing New York business attire—loafers, white shirt, blazer with gold buttons, khaki or dark green pants. I'd take my blazer off, and then I'd clean the floor, polish it up and make it look nice. And guess what? Dick liked that, a bookkeeper cleaning up his floors.

Soon enough, I'm getting to use the company car and a gas card. I'm spending weekends up in Napa Valley. And I'm learning the party rental supply business, which I'd never thought about in my life, but turned out to be quite interesting, especially for someone like me who likes to meet people and see how they live. If Taylor hadn't motivated me to take a better job, and if Dick hadn't hired me, who knows where I'd be today? Changing the way a fast food chicken chain cooks its meals? Living back with my mom on Long Island? Who can say?

That's how life works. Who can say what tomorrow—or tonight—will bring? I mentioned Gabriel, my old friend from Boston. Well, about twenty years ago, I was invited to a party. I was, as always, the first guest to arrive. Remember, I'm always punctual. So I'm alone in this two-bedroom house. There's basically no furniture, one light is on, and a few candles are burning. Loud music is playing. I thought, "Well, obviously there's going to be a party here." So I sat down and waited. Eventually, people started showing up. Guess who is one of them? Gabriel! About seven years after I'd last seen him, my friend Gabriel had made the move to California! Incredible! I said, "Hey, what's going on! Where you staying?" He said, "Oh, man, I'm staying at a hotel in Inglewood. Seven dollars per day." I said to Gabriel, "Why don't you come move in with me?"

Well, listen, I don't know if it was a good move or bad move. Since then, Gabriel has been stuck—*stuck*—

to me. Wherever someone sees Gabriel, Georges somehow is hanging around. And the other way, too. That's why people come to my restaurant and ask, "Where is Gabriel?"

You see, doors never close for us Haïtians. Once a friend, always a friend. Once we start something, we're going to stay with it, no matter how many years it takes to achieve. In fact, you can go ahead and close all the doors. We'll find a window.

Why? I think it has to do something with our education. Here we are, exposed to the French ways. The Spanish ways. African ways. Indian ways. And at church and in my case, at Catholic school, you're learning Latin, too. In Haïti, it was a must to learn a second language. You are not going to finish your schooling and not have taken either Latin or Greek or Spanish or English or Portuguese, you name it.

I'm thinking about the schooling of Haïti, how tough that was. Let me tell you: once you pass third grade in Haïti, you're beginning to have stomach pains from the pressure. Mornings, you'd have two or three books to memorize and recite. One class started at 8:00 a.m. and by 11:00 a.m., you'd break for lunch. You'd go home and be due back by 1:00 p.m. And some of the guys who went to public school, they probably had to return by 2:00 p.m. Then in the afternoon, you would have history class and civics, you would have Bible material to memorize, you would have geography to memorize, and you would have mathematics.

Let me tell you: it was tough. My brother Michael, man, this guy was so smart. He was the first guy I knew who learned to read upside-down. A guy like me, I was bright, but I was fearful. I simply could not memorize things. I'd learn all the material, but by the time I'd get to school, that'd be it—all the information I'd mashed into my brain the night prior was no longer available.

☼ ☼ ☼

ALL THESE TECHNIQUES THAT we have had to deal with early on, that's what creates the makeup of a Haïtian. We do not take schooling for granted. Those who can afford to go to school, go to school, and make the effort to learn and take the responsibility to learn.

That was the same with my cooking. Although I'd go to school, cooking techniques and recipes were the things I'd never forget.

My grandmother used to tell me, "TiGeorges, you were such a sick child. I never want you to suffer in life."

And I haven't, thanks to the education that she gave me, and the education my parents gave me, and my brothers and sisters.

Yes, the business of food—cooking and selling— very nearly killed me the day I was born.

Let me tell you: the way my life turned out, instead, cooking sustains me. The flame, the flavor, the spice, the wafting bouquet of smoking avocado wood, the sizzle of fat dripping off rotisserie chicken, the patted stomachs and dazzled smiles shared by sated customers, this is what I live for!

I, TiGeorges Laguerre—or, if you will, *Jean-Marie Monfort Hébert Georges Fils Laguerre*—I really truly live to cook. I can't wait to see you soon for a great meal in Echo Park. And, friends, please do what you can to help Haïti prosper.

Merci, mèsi, thank you, y gracias.

ABOUT THE AUTHORS AND THE ILLUSTRATOR

Jean-Marie Monfort Hébert Georges Fils "TiGeorges" Laguerre is the chef and owner of TiGeorges' Chicken, in Los Angeles, California. Laguerre is a native of Port-de-Paix, Haïti. This is his first book. For more information: www.tigeorgeschicken.com

Jeremy Rosenberg is the Assistant Dean for Public Affairs and Special Events at the USC Annenberg School for Communication and Journalism. His previous book, *Under Spring: Voices + Art + Los Angeles* (Heyday), won the first-ever California Historical Society Book Award. Rosenberg is a former employee of the *Los Angeles Times* and the Annenberg Foundation, and his words about culture, ideas, history, cuisine, policy, and more have appeared in dozens of print and online books, newspapers, magazines. He was named a Next American City Vanguard in 2009. Follow him on Twitter at @LosJeremy.

Chandler Wood is a Los Angeles based artist, specializing in comic art and storyboards. From 2005 to 2010 his *Another LA Story* ran in the *LA Weekly*.